Real Estate Investing

Table of Contents

4

Introduction

"The best investment on Earth is earth."

—**Louis Glickman**, American Real Estate Investor

Undoubtedly, real estate investing is the greatest means to earn passive income. Nevertheless, it entails a myriad of minute details that you should be aware of or learn in order to master and understand fully the business.

For one, you may even ask, ***"HOW DO I GET ROLLING IN THE WORLD OF REAL ESTATE INVESTING?"*** Although others might be leading you to believe in a plain and easy solution that suits and works for everyone, it would never be simply the case.

This real estate investing handbook will help you to streamline the various processes of figuring out how you will set out on your real estate investing journey. Along the process, you will learn how to become a successful real estate investor in the current market regardless of your present experience level, credit rating, or even how much earnings or money you have.

Apparently, the guidelines outlined herein do not represent an all-inclusive scope of about every aspect and angle in the realm of real estate investing. Instead, it presents to you a broad, yet, simplified overview of the ideal ways of how to start treading on your path towards financial freedom by investing in real estate.

Essentially, this manual consists of eight sections, each focusing on a specifically vital stage of your real estate investing adventure:

I—Learning the Basic Concepts of Real Estate Investing: Just as real estate investing constitutes a multi-faceted field, which you need to explore, you should understand everything it entails prior to even testing its waters or plunging directly into its vast ocean. The bottom line though is that it is imperative to know that investing in real estate neither needs to be expensive nor difficult nor complicated.

II—Essentials of Becoming a Real Estate Investor: Educating you or building the foundation for your real estate knowledge can detail many possible ways. You can learn the ropes on your own or from others, and grow as a full-fledged real estate investor. However, everything begins with and within YOU—your proper attitude to confront and tackle the challenges of what it takes to succeed in real estate investing.

III—Creating Your Concrete Real Estate Business Plan: You will always have greater chances of producing financial gains from the market in your real estate investing efforts. Nonetheless, these favorable possibilities can only become realities if you truly understand what you will be doing in accordance with a concrete plan you have set in place for acquiring your desired property.

Building a solid foundation from which your real estate investing endeavors will be anchoring upon will result in a stronger and more sustainable real estate investing venture that can weather all the business' storms you may encounter.

IV/V—Choosing Your Real Estate Market Niche and Strategies: A number of varying strategies are necessary to approach the real estate investing business corresponding to the diverse types of real estate properties you may utilize.

As you dive deeper into understanding the various property niches, you will learn to focus on a specific type of real estate. Likewise, you will be looking at different angles on how you can set up your chosen property on the market and how to apply its pertinent investment strategies to make a windfall from it.

VI—Finding the Ideal Properties to Invest: Your first real estate investment purchase is vitally crucial; it will either make or break your financial dreams and momentum. Learn how to set the proper parameters to guide you in making your decisions and finding for a quality property.

For all you know, you need not pay too much when purchasing your first property. Instead, you must know how to appreciate or increase its inherent value and get it after finding a property with so much potential.

VII—Applying Financing Tools on Your Property Investments: Paying for or financing your property investment is never similar to paying for some commodity. The financing vehicle or method applied can often denote the difference between failure and success in real estate investing. Know the specific financing tools that you can apply all through your property-investing career.

VIII—How to Market Your Real Estate Investments: Obviously, you should know how to manage your real estate. Foremost, this means being a good property owner to any of your tenants you wish to admit into your investment.

In addition, never rely upon the age-old adage, *"If you will build it, then they will come by and buy."* No matter what type of property investment you opt to focus on, you will definitely need a strong and persuasive marketing skill set.

8

Creating the proper marketing program, as well as allocating its compulsory resources is extremely significant towards the success of any property investment business over the long haul.

IX—Understanding and Mastering Strategies of Your Way Out: How you plan to exit or unload your real estate investments are as important as how you have first entered or landed into them.

In order to optimize your investment and minimize the risks, you should have an implicit outlook of your exit strategy options—to either sell or trade or, rent your property out. Know the market and identify its needs so you can chart the proper course for your real estate investment programs.

If you can only muster and master learning all these, then you will be stepping up your chances of creating passive wealth through real estate. Alongside, you will be reducing the risks of losses or failures in your property investment plans.

By this informative guide, it will help you to learn real estate investing from start to end with no exaggerated claims, extravagant pitches, and false promises. The entire learning process might take you weeks or even months to accomplish or put into effect.

Strive to persevere though; after all, you cannot afford to compromise your real estate investment. As much as possible, show your seriousness by knowing what to do with those promising property deals that can work out to your advantage.

Work harder towards establishing yourself into the real estate market. Care for your brand and brand it with care!

While staying engaged through this manual, remember that this does not embrace every aspect of property investing. Rather, it unveils a comprehensive review and summary of how real estate investing functions while presenting you with the fundamental tools for moving ahead from the persistent question of how to start out and get going.

"Real estate can neither be lost nor stolen nor can it be carried away. Purchased with common sense, paid for in full, and managed with reasonable care, it is about the safest investment in the whole wide world."

—Franklin D. Roosevelt, 32nd President of the U.S.A.

1-Fundamental Concepts of Real Estate Investing

"It's tangible, it's solid, and it's beautiful. It's artistic from my standpoint, and I just love real estate."

—**Donald Trump**, 45th President of the U.S.A.

The universal concept of investing in real estate has been flourishing since time immemorial. In essence, real estate investing is a business practice wherein you acquire a home, or a lot or land, or another property, which you could hold onto for a prolonged period.

By its technical aspect, and just as most people perceive it to be, real estate investing is simply the buying and selling of a property. Nevertheless, unlike other forms of business investments, property investors hold a sense of authority and control over what they possess.

In other instances, real estate investors can possibly gain complete control over the present structures, including the entire land of the entailed property. Such a full authority adds up to the value or asset that investors will have for their usage and disposition.

The general objective of real estate investing is selling a property at a profit in the future. Therefore, it would be necessary for you to find feasible ways of selling your property soon after its value appreciates. However, the definite or proper time by which to sell your property depends on numerous factors and other industry forces that can influence the real estate market directly.

The best part in real estate investing is its flexible opportunities. You can always participate in the acquisition of any type of property available that can work for you.

The real estate market does not limit you to finding only a traditional house and lot. It can also let you obtain a larger industrial space or commercial building that might catch your fancy. Thus, whatever it is you desire, you can certainly avail it on the market today and earn exciting gains from your investment.

While real estate investing may be a controversial choice for earning passive income, you should be aware of the associated risks in entering, possessing, and holding out a real estate investment. Be advised that your property investment plans and engagements have no guarantees of resulting in a profit. All the properties on the market may be subject to risks of depreciation or losing their par value.

Furthermore, be sensible and discerning of the assets you own on hand prior to participating in a real estate investment. Depending on what you plan to utilize for your property investment whims, the expenses involved may be too steep. Be guided at what real estate investing is and what it is not. More importantly, know what you ought to need to get started:

Why Invest in Real Estate?

You can have so many different investment options for growing your money lest sticking it under your bed. The most common preferences include bank savings, bonds or lending, certificates of deposit (CD's), commodities trading/exchange-traded products (ETPs)/futures contracts, foreign currency trading (FOREX), mutual or hedge funds, and stocks.

Yet, the most promising of these investment choices is property or real estate investment. The only common denominator for all these investment vehicles is having their respective pros and cons.

Anybody can engage in real estate investing and there is no other proper time to learn how but now! Property values, especially throughout the U.S. are much lower than ever during the last half of the century. This may be old news to you, but what is likely new news for you is the financial expectation of capitalizing from the prevailing low prices and purchasing real estate at enormous discounts while you are still able.

Perhaps, it could be understandable that you still somehow feel apprehensive over the 2007-2009 bursting of the U.S. real estate bubble, including the mortgage meltdown that ensued. Just the same, reserve precious time to educate yourself about the benefits and advantages of property investing and you will soon discover that you will no longer have to be so agitated.

Among the most common reasons people declare for engaging in real estate investing is to seek out a continuous and sustainable financial freedom. However, there are other motives as well just as each individual will always have their own personal decisions and convictions.

Typically, you can seek one or a couple or more of the following reasons why you should invest in real estate:

❖ **Alternatives or Options:** Some investors confess to classifying property investing as nothing more than a segment under their investment portfolio umbrella. For this reason, they only look forward to achieving higher rates of returns from their cash investments through implementing an active management.

Others have come to realize loving and enjoying real estate investing because it provided them with so many more options (i.e., choices to keep traveling, purchasing, working, etc.). Besides, the more they invest in, the more windows of opportunity open up for them.

Appreciation/Equity Creation: An increased property value comes along over time. Usually, appreciated values stem from either a natural appreciation in the market or whatever improvements implemented to the property (i.e., structural enhancements, repairs, and remodeling).

Sometimes, the property value can also appreciate whenever a substantial number of tenants avail the property. Besides a sufficient occupancy rate, longer tenancy durations can also result in creating equity and increasing the value on the property.

Other investors would rather relate the thrills of the chase of hunting down a rosy property deal or their latest remodeled property. These investors pursue such habit-forming attitude and feeling while being always on the lookout for the subsequent opportunity of transforming an ugly duckling into a comely swan.

Continuous Cash Flow: Acquiring real estate—whether through an all-cash purchase or paying through the currently favorable financing modes of low mortgage amortizations—will yield positive cash flows monthly. The steady monthly income occurs after deducting the monthly loan defrayal from the property's monthly rental.

In comparison, investing in most paper assets does not yield a positive monthly cash flow. Instead, you are investing for capital gains income, which actually incurs higher tax payments.

Besides, paper assets will never provide you with any gains, especially when the national economy performs poorly. Hence, you may lose easily your investment or a bigger percentage of it.

When investing in cash flow, your property's value is immaterial. Your return on investment (ROI) will rather manifest clearly on the cash flow.

Additionally, you will not incur the risks of losing your property or initial investment regardless of the prevailing national economic conditions. Economic fluctuations will not likely affect your property investments if you come prepared.

Preparedness implies creating a cash flow stream involving multiple asset categories. This will put you in a safer financial position where the cash flow covers your monthly expenses. If ever your expenditures increase along with rising inflation, your cash flow also increases due to rental inflation.

🏠 **Complete Control:** Real estate investing bestows you with certain levels of control over your financial plans. Fact is that you will have nary any control over financial investments other than in real estate.

Many financial managers will suggest diversifying your investments in paper assets, specifically CD's or mutual funds. The hidden hitch is that as you engage more with these low-risk investments, you are actually increasing the risk levels by investing exclusively in them. Still, your main issue here is having no control whatsoever over the value of the asset because you could neither improve on its value nor renovate it as you would in real estate investing.

By investing in real estate, you can readily control the risks of your property. Such controls could be through shielding the property from economic fluctuations through a positive periodic cash flow, applying it with the appropriate insurance, forming it with a legal business structure (i.e., partnership or other creative business entity structuring), or equipping it with multiple exit strategies that augment increasing the ROI while reducing the risks.

🏠 **Inflation Protection:** When there is an occurrence of a persistent increase in consumer price levels or a persistent decline in the consumers' purchasing power, real estate assets bear protections from such states of inflation. Normally, real estate values can appreciate despite no changes in its demand; thus, they can withstand the effects of inflation or a weak currency.

On the contrary, the worth of paper assets primarily remains the same while everything else shoots up their value. Hence, real estate investors who ably cope with inflation leave paper asset investors in the dust, losing larger sums of money during periods of slow economic growths.

🏠 **Career Interest/Escape/Shift:** Many real estate investors perceive property investing as a chance of owning their own business or a major career shift. Some even consider real estate as an instrument of replacing ultimately the career or job they hate.

Others dive into real estate investing head on—akin to lemmings jumping off cliffs—instead of intending the investment falling squarely on their shoulders. Whichever preference you may look at it, engaging with its profitable investing activities compels you to learn along the way and hurdle the obstacles.

Leveraged Usage of Credit or Borrowed Funds: Real estate investing gives you the power to use your limited assets to guarantee a considerable amount of loan necessary to finance your investment. Say, you acquired a property worth $100,000 through a bank loan of 80%. That means your cash outlay would be $20,000 at the close.

Assuming the property appreciated by $5,000 within a year, your $20,000 initial payment will yield an equity increase of $25,000, or a 25% ROI in a year. If you further apply other real estate investing benefits to the property (i.e., a monthly rental cash flow), then the increased appreciation would even be much higher.

Hence, when applying this powerful purchasing advantage properly, you can borrow finances conveniently against your investment and have the chance to increase more your ROI. Rarely can you use such advantage when investing in paper assets; it is risky since you will have no control over paper investments.

Tax Benefits/Depreciation: A reduced value or depreciation on a property is common to real estate. Yet, real estate investing uncommonly benefits from depreciation since a property acquisition cost is high; and oftentimes, obtained with debt. The Internal Revenue System (IRS) acknowledges that assets can wear down over time, thus, using this depreciation factor in its tax laws.

Somehow, the IRS evaluated that residential properties wear down exactly within 27.5 years. Thus, if you invest in real estate, you receive depreciation benefits equivalent to about 60% to 80% of the acquisition cost divided by 27.5 years.

Even if a property appreciates, the national government incredibly provides owners certain tax deductions on their properties across their lifetimes. You can even claim the interests in your monthly mortgage payments as tax-deductible items.

For instance, if you acquire real estate for $100,000, then the IRS writes off $60,000 (depending on the property value) across 27.5 years. This means you will receive a tax deduction of $2,181 on whatever income your property creates.

Hence, if you earn $6,000 per annum in rental income, then you would only be paying taxes pegged on $3,819 in lieu of the originally designated $6,000. These tax deductions are huge as opposed to other forms of investments. Paper asset incomes do not even carry any tax benefits.

Financial predators like the IRS will usually find more ways of taxing you. Therefore, match their responsibility by also finding more ways for reducing those tax payments.

Real estate investing is one route to unburden you from the government's tax impositions. With a reduction in your tax payments, it only implies a facilitation of moving ahead financially.

Is Property Investing Viable While Engaged in a Full-Time Job?

The truth of the matter is that there are a hundred and one ways to earn income from real estate. Many of these methods might require you spending 30 hours or more per week, while some techniques might only necessitate you working 30 hours or less per year. The growth rate of your real estate business actually depends on your skill sets, personality, strategies, and plans.

If your desired career path would be to migrate to the Maldives and teach vacationers to dive or launch an environmental campaign for the preservation of endangered species, then forget about becoming a full-time investor. This does not denote that you should no longer engage in real estate investing; probably, you just should not go full time.

Nevertheless, you need not establish real estate as your career for building your wealth solely from it. If you truly love your full-time job, then you need not even quit so you can focus on real estate investing.

Actually, you can achieve similar, if not, much better results as a full-time employee while investing in real estate on the side. One benefit that dominates when investing in real estate while working full time is enjoying a stream of steady income to finance or support your investment programs.

Furthermore, you will have many advantages over full-time real estate investors when keeping your day job or working full-time. Foremost, your cash flow gained from real estate investing need not sustain your subsistence. Your 9-to-5 job will foot the bill for your everyday existence.

For this reason, you have greater chances of reinvesting all the income from your property investments. In no time, you will realize fully the incredible gains of exponential profits and growth.

Indeed, a stable income from your regular job would certainly augment stabilizing and developing further your wealth-building plans. You will even have an easy ability for securing loans or grow the required capacities for procuring long-term bank financing.

Generally, you can choose from the following most commonly used methods to invest in real estate while keeping your regular full-time job:

🏠 **Equity Partnership in the Acquisition of Huge Pieces of Property**

🏠 **Property Management under a Buy-And-Hold Setup**

❖ **Serving To Be A Hard Money Lender or As A Private Money Financier**

🏠 **Investing In Mortgage Notes**

🏠 **Investing In Tax Lien Certificates**

Either as your full-time career or as a sideline from your day job, real estate investing can be greatly profitable. Nonetheless, the proper path to take is all your choice.

Just because you have read or heard about the success of others investing in real estate, you should not quickly decide to end your employment to follow their lead and pursue working full-time into real estate investing. It is essential to have a solid real estate investing plan on how you are going to proceed with towards investing in real estate.

For all that, life becomes too short when you are stuck in a job you abhorred. Discern choosing a career path that energizes and excites you from sunrise to sunset and lets you feel more than contented when falling asleep. If your dream path leads you to invest full-time in real estate, just ensure that you are not simply building your career, but rather, building your future.

Are Real Estate Mentors a Necessity Towards Success?

Legions of real estate investors have achieved success without the guidance or help from so-called mentors or advisers. More often than not, the objective of these characters is to prey on gullible people, hooking them on the dreams of easy money and getting rich quickly. Usually, they employ slick tactics of selling expensive training courses, webinars, boot camps, etc.

Bear in mind that many have also somehow benefitted from some of these self-styled experts and their marketing ploys. Most of the investment niche websites ride on their bandwagon by affiliating with them. These sites earn huge referral fees, usually a 50%-cut on orders, for marketing their mentoring programs, events, and other products.

Given that, some seasoned real estate gurus are not as notorious as others are. They are very knowledgeable with their first-hand experiences and long exposures of living the life before. Fact is that they are even generous enough to share with a newbie or you a tip or two.

Finding pride and fulfillment to pass on to others their legacy is one main cause why they come approaching you to teach with the ways and byways of real estate. Other reasons may be having a company with mutual interests to talk with; or perhaps, simply seeing potentials of negotiating future property deals with you.

These organic mentorships, commonly known as 'friendships,' occur from day to day. Although they are oftentimes misunderstood, looking for your real estate mentors and learning from them are among the most significant primary steps you should take, especially in educating you in real estate investing.

Just remember always the business principle, *'caveat emptor'*—you alone must bear the risks for the quality of a purchase before buying; never assume that the assessed quality comes with a guarantee. Do your own homework. Never allow yourself entangled and ensnared in hyped-up promises of business secrets, as there is really none in the first place.

Would It Be Possible Investing in Real Estate without Money?

Even if you do not have the wherewithal, it would still be possible to engage in real estate investing. Nonetheless, every real estate investment deal involves money.

Therefore, the issue is not about investing with *NO MONEY*. Rather, it is investing with *NOTHING OF YOUR OWN MONEY*.

Real estate investing using none of your own finances compels you to use **'other people's money (OPM).'** OPM is important, yet, a complicated investing tool to use.

Your only key is to offer or provide a useful attribute or skill to the negotiating table. If you really have deficient finances, you can always bring to the table your time, education, knowledge, common sense or intelligence, confidence, creativity, and a network of connections.

After you complete reading this manual, you would have already taken big strides towards creating your strengths in those attributes. Several investors use only a little to nothing of their own money in real estate investing by applying any of the following acquisition techniques:

- Equity Partnership Agreement

- Lease Option Techniques

- Lines Of Credit or Home Equity Loans

- Wholesaling of Real Estate

- Hard Money/Private Money

- **Zero Down Payment Loans** (i.e. private lender-issued VA loan or the U. S. Veteran Affairs guaranteed loan)

- **Low Upfront Fee Loans** (i.e., 2.75%-down payment USDA loan or the U.S. Department of Agriculture Rural Development Guaranteed Housing Loan Program and the 3.5%-down payment Federal Housing Administration [FHA] loan)

Other would-be real estate investors have never invested any money at all. They get to start and earn their spurs by simply working while learning hands-on within the real estate industry.

You can learn the business like the palm of your hand by pursuing and mastering any of these careers: appraiser, construction worker, escrow/title agent, mortgage broker, property manager, or real estate agent. The experiences you will gain from any of these industry trades are invaluable; they will help you to begin plotting your full-time career in real estate investing.

Is Real Estate Investing a Formula to Get Rich Quickly?

Undoubtedly, images and scenes of real estate investors living in posh mansions, driving fancy cars, and kowtowing with the rich and famous are among the great drawing powers of real estate investing. Truly, the field of real estate has fountains of money.

Although several real estate investors have created enormous wealth over their careers and lifetime, real estate investing is categorically NOT a get-rich-quickly-scheme. A fortunate few might have made a significant windfall within a short span of time, but these circumstances are often exceptions instead of the rule.

In reality, real estate investing necessitates you to exercise its all-important *3Ps—Persistence, Patience, and Planning*. Know that there are neither tools nor products that will be doing all the work for you; neither shortcuts will help you to succeed in real estate investing.

Regardless of what you hear or see otherwise, you need hard work to succeed just as any other fields of endeavor require. Never expect to earn a million bucks within your initial year of the undertaking. Instead, plan to build a real estate business that will grow steadily through the years to allow yourself meeting your emotional security and financial affluence, independence, goals, and ultimately, your dreams.

"Ninety percent of all millionaires become so through owning real estate. Real estate has created more money than in all industrial investments combined. The wise young man or wage earner of today invests his money in real estate."

—**Andrew Carnegie**, Scottish-American Industrialist & Philanthropist

2-Laying the Foundations of Real Estate Investing

"Now, one thing I tell everyone is to learn about real estate investing. Repeat after me: real estate provides the highest returns, the greatest values, and the least risk."

—**Armstrong Williams**, American Entrepreneur & Political Analyst

Having a good grasp on the basic principles of investing in real estate will develop the solid foundation of your real estate education. They will be guiding your way in avoiding imminent risks of losses and failures in your future transactions. If you have to remember only a single portion of this handbook to prepare yourself in launching your real estate investing journey, this is the most indispensable section.

For your information, you need not pay hefty amounts to learn all the intricacies and details of the business. In the first place, you will have countless different ways to educate yourself in real estate investing. You might exhaust all your finances paying your education before acquiring your first real estate property!

Primarily, you could begin your real estate education by reading pertinent books and blogs or listening to informative podcasts and other live audio programs. Alternatively, you can get yourself under the tutelage of a good mentor.

You might think that what easily works for others may not truly work for you. Just the same, choose the best and most convenient method where you feel you can develop and begin learning quickly.

As a primer, nonetheless, you just ought to master this ensuing couple of principles of real estate investing education. Always ensure applying each of this pair of fundamental lessons prior to your decision of proceeding on your investment plans:

Essential Real Estate Mathematics

Doing the math in real estate is no more complicated than in 10th grade. Everything is as easy as counting 1-2-3! You need not be a college student adept at solving algebraic expressions and integral calculus equations to learn real estate arithmetic and math formulas.

The following simple terminologies and concepts, as well as their sample calculations, will lay the foundation on which all other real estate computations derive and relate their equations. Worry not about the rest of those self-perceived complex formulas; you will eventually learn them in time.

🏠 **Income** – is the amount of money you receive or direct profit that comes in during a definite period from your property investment. The math involved under this term is probably the easiest: you simply add up the property's proceeds.

For instance, you own a rental property, which rents for $1,500 a month. Your tenant also pays an extra $30 monthly for using the garage. Therefore, your total income in a month's time will be $1,530.

Income can also denote extra payments such as application/down payment amounts, late rental penalty dues, topped up utility fees, pet charges, or any other additional values and payables you receive from your property's monthly rental.

⌂ Expenses – are particular items, which necessarily cost you money from your property investment. For instance, you spend $60 for your property's monthly garbage collection billing; an allocated $90 for its monthly maintenance; and, a $550 monthly loan payment to your bank. Therefore, your total expenditure for the month is $700.

Expenses can come unexpected, fixed, or variable per month. Being a real estate investor, you should know and prepare your finances to face these obligations, which include insurance payments, capital expenses, tax duties, holding costs, management fees, etc.

⌂ Cash Flow – is the remaining amount of money or ending balance at month's end after paying all the expenses. You simply deduct your total expenses from your total income to determine your cash flow. Therefore, your total cash flow for the month based on the aforementioned examples is $830.00.

⌂ Return on Investment (ROI) – is only a sophisticated term for describing the interest rate you earn per annum on your startup capital. For instance, if you invested initially $1,000 and profited $1,000 (or a total ending balance of $2,000) from your investment within a year, you earned a 100% ROI.

Similarly, if you committed an initial capital of $2,000 and gained $1,000 (or a total ending balance of $3,000) from your investment within a year, you earned a 50% ROI.

In the simplest terms, you compute for your ROI as expressed in this formula: $(B_2 - B_1) \div B_1 = ROI$, whereby, B_2 is the total ending balance while B_1 is the initial capital or beginning balance.

Ways of Becoming a Successful Real Estate Investor: Reinventing Your Mindset

A major roadblock in your eventual real estate journey is fear. Almost all the successful real estate investors have experienced certain levels of fear, or perhaps, skepticisms while entering into or negotiating a property deal. In all possibilities, you are having feelings of apprehension and disquiet, as well as fear, especially when you are just about to get weaving in real estate investing.

You do not have to worry. On one hand, it is normal for us to feel fear, as fear itself is natural. On the other hand, fear helps us in a way to avoid wrong decisions, including those consequences stemming therefrom.

Nevertheless, fear can also be overwhelming that it can stop you dead on your tracks, immobilizing you from making your next step forward. In effect, you will simply be spinning your wheels without ever progressing.

As a resolve, you should address your fears right from the start. Hereunder are confidence-building measures for overcoming your fears and helping you to succeed in spite of its presence:

🏠 **Stimulation and Systemization**: If you finally decide to replace the job, which you truly hate, with a real estate investing career, then you had better get off your ass and start working on it. Plan to organize your work, and work on your organized plan.

Commit yourself to your work, to hard work, and to your actions. Never allow mediocrity to set in. Do not bask immediately in newfound, yet, temporal glories. Step up on your momentum. Identify your standards and create benchmarks on your deals.

Never settle for anything less; you always deserve something better. Keep learning along the way to enhance your real estate education. Stop purchasing costly and media-hyped real estate training programs and their course materials.

As much as possible, avoid seeking out real estate coaches until you are certain enough to make real estate investing your full-time career. Without a firm commitment, neither courses nor mentors will bring and lead you closer to your objective.

Most of these lectures and courses usually focus on technical aspects, hypothetical situations, and assumed thoughts. For all you know, the real brewing action occurs inside what the grey matter between your ears cooks up.

Trust yourself and your thoughts. Draw in the reins over your thoughts and emotions, and stay under control. Actually, it never matters what strategy you apply for as long as you know and will to deal with the different issues involved. Else, you will just waste your time, money, and efforts.

Participate in Productive Programs: Social networks and online forums focused on real estate investing are teeming with expert investors who are more than willing to share freely their knowledge. Create your account and try to participate daily.

These are also avenues to learn more in-depth references of real estate education. Do not be afraid to ask questions, even those queries perceived to be clichés. Your questions, regardless of what they may be, are of great concerns to you. Remember, you have to educate yourself as comprehensively as you can. Otherwise, you will just be as afraid speaking with property sellers or negotiating with major developers.

Human relations will play a principal role in your life as a real estate investor. Never stay idle; interact with like-minded people, build goodwill with them, and nurture your relationships. Allowing yourself to be visible to your colleagues at all times—offline or online—ensures your presence at the forefront of their consciousness. That would be greatly helpful to your business!

🏠 **Learn the Language**: Grow your confidence by learning to speak the real estate lingoes and jargons. Especially when you find yourself in unfamiliar dialogues, you should be up to standard and follow the lead of those who are conversant or know the ropes. As they say, *"When in Rome, do as the Romans do!"*

Otherwise, you will develop self-perceptions of professional inferiority and skepticism. You will always become shy and afraid that you may act and sound as if you are clueless in your conversations.

Certainly, as soon as you can build your confidence in speaking and understanding the language of the trade, you will enhance your speaking ability in discussing with others or the insiders of the industry. Besides, speaking the same language becomes a catalyst to facilitate transactions and speed up negotiations.

🏠 **Clarify Concepts**: Apart from becoming acquainted with real estate speech and communication, you need to understand and explain adequately common terminological definitions and certain industry concepts (i.e., the importance of 70% after-repair-value [ARV] in flipping, debt-to-income ratio, etc.).

Being unclear gives rise to fear. Refer further to Section 5 to gain more knowledge by discovering more real estate conceptual terms.

As a tip, try imparting your knowledge of these unfamiliar terms to someone else. In this way, you are unconsciously etching those concepts in mind, enabling you to know them by rote.

👜 **Observe Others**: Assimilate yourself with like-minded investors and simulate your bearing with how they execute their activities and methodologies in their dealings. Sooner than later, you will begin to pick up impulsively on their desirable traits and qualities that distinguish their success.

If such assimilations and simulations imply requiring you to work without any fees even during the weekends or late nights for a local investor, then accept it as the price you pay for joining the club. You will learn to overcome your fears faster when helping others to accomplish success.

'Fear' is just actually one part of the principal twin obstacles in real estate investing. *'Paralysis by analyses'* completes the duo.

Interchangeably termed as *'analysis paralysis,'* paralysis by analyses is the state when you overthink or over-analyze a situation to seek out optimal solutions until realizing in the end that you have already lost the chance of reaching a decision, making a choice, or taking action. In short, the sheer quantities of analyses you provided overwhelm the decision-making process itself. As a result, you paralyze entirely the outcome.

Usually, analysis paralysis occurs during moments when you plan, research, and evaluate in endless cycles. It also manifests when you meet others without interacting, read blogs without engaging, and read books without implementing. Typically, this is all due to your fears of making any outright decisions, which could result in erroneous circumstances.

31

It would be easier convincing yourself that you have no inklings on everything you ought to know prior to begin taking action. Nevertheless, you need not learn about each real estate strategy for every niche. Much less, you neither have to be an expert nor a seasoned investor before getting yourself to work hard.

You only need to concentrate first on a single field of real estate investing, and then, work your way into becoming an expert with it. Learn one investing field at a time. Once you recognize where you wish to pursue, learn everything you ever need to know on it.

Then again, you just might feel unprepared to begin. You will most likely never begin unless you take action.

Fear can strike again while you start. You would not be up and able to respond to all the questions asked by both buyers and sellers. However, since you took action, you dispose yourself compelling to learn the answers to all those questions.

In hindsight, all these actions taken to reduce or eliminate the attacks of fear, escalations of conflict, or transmissions of an impasse in your real estate investment activities will build your confidence of starting your course of action on your own. The quicker you can overcome all your fears, the greater the chances of your success!

> *"In any market, in any country, there are always developers who make money. So I say all of this doom and gloom, but there will always be people who make money because people always want homes."*
>
> —**Sarah Beeny**, English TV Host & Property Developer

3-Building the Real Estate Investment Business Plan

"In my experience in the real estate business, past success stories are generally not always applicable to new situations. We must reinvent continually ourselves, responding to changing times with innovative new business plans and models."

—**Akira Mori**, Japanese Real Estate Developer

Majestic buildings never sit firmly on solid foundations alone; but more significantly, they stand tall on careful and conscientious planning long before groundbreaking. Building a business plan must be integral in your real estate investing endeavors. It makes the great difference between early failure and success.

Your business plan shall serve as your vital roadmap to guide you in navigating your way towards a successful real estate journey. Foremost, it should give you an overview of the conventional routes where you can cruise along or cut corners, the common pitfalls and hidden hazards you want to avoid, and those unpredictable crossroads to watch out along the path.

Sometimes, these intersections have boulevards that deceptively lead you to broken dreams. Other times, these seemingly misleading avenues inconspicuously direct you towards your desired destination.

Therefore, as you prepare for your long-term success and grand entrance in property investing, focus on your options in building your plan. Not only will you learn planning your offers for a deal but also, visualizing events prior to placing them on the market.

Basic Elements of Your Real Estate Business Plan

When structuring your real estate investment plan, you should bear in mind to integrate the fundamental elements that would define clearly your purpose for engaging in the real estate industry. Your plan should also include the benefits that your business and these following elements provide:

🏠 **Setting-Up Goals |Mission Statement:** Draw a strong vision and come out with a rallying mission statement. Both will play as your underlying goals and intents that would chart your real estate investing path.

Over time though, your goals may change since ideals also change and are oftentimes unreal in real life. Changes in your goals may affect your entire business plan, but you need not worry.

Somehow, it is always better to be able to illustrate and see for yourself what could be the possible ways of realizing your goals and what could be not. You just have to restructure your plan with respect to the changes.

Always have a mental imagery or visualization about the future of your investment business. Ensure to list down both of your short- and long-term goals. Be realistic, but never be afraid to keep reaching for them.

By setting more achievable or smaller goals, it helps you to remain more motivated. Along your way, you will surely form a habit of always looking forward to accomplishing something.

As a quick guide to help you recognize or shape your goals, ask yourself the following questions about your destination, visualization, and timeline, and then, document your answers:

✓ What particular _real estate market niche_ do I like?

✓ What specific destination do I want to go?

✓ What do I want the real estate industry help me to achieve?

✓ What shall be the timeframe to reach finally my goal?

✓ What would be a viable and ideal succeeding 10 years look like?

✓ Would I want to call it quits after 10 years?

✓ Would I decide to quit my full-time job?

🏠 **Picking & Mastering A Real Estate Investing Strategy**: As previously mentioned, real estate investing offers you a multitude of ways to earn money; but, you need not need or know them all. It would rather be sensible to pick a single strategy and master it.

Your chosen strategy, if reliable, will become your vehicle for carrying you through towards reaching your destination or realizing your goals. Mastering an investment strategy means knowing how you are going to manage your deals or how you are going to turn a property acquisition into profits.

Make a clear definition of your investment management steps. Ensure to document all the sources of your expenses and income while preparing for the unexpected. Your preparation may also let you identify your exit strategies if ever your investment did not work out as planned.

🏠 **Building the Real Estate Marketing Plan**: You will need a system of real estate marketing for so many beneficial reasons. First, is to attract motivated sellers or let them come knocking at your door. Second, is to find the best deals listed in the market.

The real estate industry itself presents multiple ways to search for these auspicious deals. You may use the multiple listing services, online searches, services of real estate agents, direct mailing lists, etc.

Hence, your marketing plan should let you identify the most feasible method/s you will use in finding your deals. Besides, it must allow you to be flexible in altering your market niche and/or strategy if you are having difficulties of not finding enough deals.

🏠 **Establishing Parameters in Real Estate Acquisition:** Prior to starting your search for propitious deals, you should establish a set of rules or criteria to categorize those deals. Define clearly and understand fully this indispensable element of your plan.

Specify distinctly your cash flow or financing requirements, maximum allowable purchase amounts, or redevelopment budgets. Additionally, know the optimal timeframe for holding out your investments prior to exiting.

More importantly, understand your deal's *'loan-to-value (LTV)'* ratio—the amount of potential money lent with respect to the lender's appraised valuation of the property, expressed in percentage. Most lenders require a maximum LTV ratio of 75%. This implies paying out-of-pocket 25% of the property's value.

Several new investors fall into the emotional trap of getting excited or having strong affinities to certain properties that they immediately purchase or acquire the first deal coming their way. With clearly defined criteria to stick to, you will be able to take your emotions away and out of the picture; and thereby, nurture the ability to reject easily 99% of unfavorable real estate deals.

🏠 <u>Choosing the Proper Financing Vehicle to Acquire Deals</u>: Describe honestly your current financial situation so that you will know what to bring on the negotiating table. Do you wish to start investing in nothing? Do you have available equities to use?

Update and document your financial status as frequently as it changes. It is always important to know your available resources for immediate use when you proceed with your investments.

Finding financing in today's market is oftentimes an overwhelming challenge that can forestall your investment actions. By recognizing your finances, you can plan on how to acquire your deals by availing the most appropriate financing tool for you.

🏠 <u>Creating the Backup Plans & Exit Strategies</u>: Plan on how you will unload or sell your deals at a profit by making a clear outline of your exit strategies. Especially for novice investors, always learn the proper moves of your end game.

While you can always pick your preferred technique of earning income from real estate, you should know which among these techniques could generate the optimal income for your deal. One helpful way to identify your best exit strategy is to bird-dog or following closely the current movements of the market.

Building a Winning Real Estate Investing Team

Integral to your real estate investment business plan is to form your team of collaborators. This includes devising the working systems on which your team members must follow to automate and streamline all your tasks. For, after all, it is close to impossible wearing several different hats and become a one-man army in the industry.

Instead, become an armchair general, directing and delegating battle plans to your troop of able foot soldiers. Investors, especially those with larger property investment portfolios or involved in very dynamic investment activities like house flipping, usually rely daily on the complemental efforts of their team.

A consistent production of effective and efficient workflows is the most significant requisite when relying on your team. A single failure from your team member will jeopardize the entire endeavor, to the extent of destroying altogether your team's objectives.

Your team must avoid excuses and inferior work results at all costs. Otherwise, it pulls the plug of your operations; and thus, giving you losses faster than you can ever think.

Ideal workhorses for your team should exhibit great qualities and specific skills. Sometimes, it would be difficult to see these work traits on the surface lest these prospective team members become referrals from trusted associates.

Most of the time, you can see the manifestations of these desirable work behaviors by engaging in long conversations with these candidates. Your immediate parameters to watch out are their communication and interpersonal skills, work expertise, availability, work ethics, professionalism, and integrity.

Truly, you cannot assemble your team overnight or in one sitting. Your team is actually a cast of people working in various fields of businesses. Choose them carefully; they are the individuals whom you can muster towards facilitating your investing plans of moving smoothly forward and rely on for support in the realization of your real estate investing dreams (refer to Image-1):

TEAM MEMBER	SPECIFIC ROLE PARAMETRIC DETERMINANTS
Family or Friends	never pursue your investment plans until getting the full support of your family or friends
Mentor | Guide	training under the watchful tutelage of someone more knowledgeable than you can only get you wiser
Real Estate Attorney	knowledgeable in reviewing your contracts and the legalities of all your actions; agrees compensations thru fees gained from asset acquisition/disposition
Mortgage Broker	experienced in working with other investors, creative, and smart to let you avail and extend loans; has the ability to provide a list of buyers/lease purchasers
Certified Public Accountant	preferably one who also owns rental properties, to perform bookkeeping works and tax management (especially, executing *'write-offs'* or reducing/cancelling a property's book value)
Insurance Agent	handles real estate insurance policies (i.e., protecting you from losses due to acts of nature or other events that damage your property; maintaining records; managing policy renewals; and, settling claims)
Building Contractor or Architect	licensed, bonded, and insured builder responsible for providing supervision, equipment, materials, and labor needed to construct, install, repair, remodel, or renovate your property; preferably, one who gets things done on time and within budget
Realtor | Real Estate Agent	punctual, eager, and enterprising resource for contract real estate works (i.e., bird-dogging markets and prospects, referring buyers/renters, showing properties, supervising open houses, rendering broker comparisons/price opinions, etc.); paid from the commission of selling a property
Escrow Officer or Title Representative	skillful negotiator or deal-closer who always looks out for your interests *'from-the-offer-to-getting-the-keys'* *(applicable only to certain areas using escrow)*
Property Manager	manage property efficiently by surveying and establishing rental rates; computing overhead costs, depreciation, taxes, and profit goals; advertising vacancies or obtaining referrals from current tenants; explaining advantages of location and services; and, showing the property for inspection
Handyman	perform skillfully your various day-to-day small tasks

Image-1: General Composition of a Real Estate Winning Team

Your best chance of sourcing the brightest members aboard your team is through referrals from your fellow investors. Generally, these investors would be feeling proud and happy to refer their own set of team players to you since it can reflect satisfactorily on themselves, as well as their relationships with those professionals.

Business Partnerships & Entity Structuring

Another essential to your real estate investment business plan is to decide whether you want to embark on your investing career by having along a business partner or simply going solo. Whatever your decision, it is never the same for everybody. It depends largely on your accumulated knowledge or experiences, time commitments or work schedules, and investment timeline plans.

If you decide to work under a partnership structure, then it would be important to consider also the nature of your intended partnership. Ensure choosing a partner who can add value to your relationship, exercise fair business practices to treat you fairly, communicate regularly, and maintain pursuing relative goals as yours. Plan carefully your arrangement in writing.

If you decide to work without a partner, you are actually not working alone. Instead of sharing 50% of your profits, you may simply outsource helping hands that can deliver certain tasks that you are not skilled to perform or, simply hate to do.

For instance, if you have no skills or knowledge in construction works, then it may be much cheaper hiring a building contractor than entering into a partnership with someone proficient with construction. This goes the same way with assembling your team. Outsource only those specialized professionals whom you think have the skillful abilities to do jobs better than you do.

PARTNERSHIP PROS	PARTNERSHIP CONS
Mutual Brainstorming: Two heads are better than one; so, as multiple minds work through similar issues, ideas often develop with more focus and clearer direction.	**Clash of Personalities:** Differences in personalities can lead to conflicts, especially when partners never jive well in relying with each other and accomplishing things.
Pooling of Resources: Generally, real estate investing involves larger resources that can be too expensive for a single person to handle. Partnerships allow pooling each other's resources to get on a stable start. Ideally, banks prefer financing to solid partnerships.	**Differences in Opinions:** Each individual has a different opinion of how to do things. As a result, differing opinions compel one to compromise on many aspects of the business—from the choices of paint color to the type of investment to pursue. If not, conflicts will most likely ensue.
Accurate Analyses: Analysis can entail several considerations upon searching for a property deal or observing the market. Conferring and comparing each other's evaluations will increase odds of accurate analyses.	**Trust Issues:** Similar to close relationships, trust issues easily arise, especially when things get rough. Trust can be hard to gain and quick to lose. Fraud can also play a role in the meltdown of many business partnerships.
Complemental Efforts: Partnerships bring complemental strengths and weaknesses—time vs. knowledge, construction vs. financing, or analytical vs. hands-on). Successful partnerships recognize each other's qualities and harness combined efforts.	**Delayed Decisions:** Acting alone tends to make quick decisions based on personal preferences. Partnerships often force to discuss every decision—whether major or trivial—and thus, leading to long delays in business transactions.
Split Risk: All investments entail certain levels of risk. Partnerships split the risks (as the profits) and lessen fears of losses.	**Lesser Profits:** Bounded by an agreement, partners split profits. Obviously, partners earn much lesser per deal than solo investors do.
Broader Network Base: Partners come to the table with their own wide network of connections within and outside the industry that can provide a business edge in so many ways.	**Mixing Affinities with Business:** Partnerships that usually involve family/friends do not always work out due to attached emotions, which often prevail midst critical decision-makings.
Built-In Accountability: Partners working out their roles create a built-in accountability, which helps moving the business forward. As one falters, the other steps in to assist, keeping the team to move on.	**Shared Responsibility:** One is responsible for the other for each business dealing, as well as any legal ramifications that can stem from it. Both partners are still responsible even if one skips town to avoid culpability.
Confidence/Motivation: Partners inspire motivation and confidence midst crises.	**Unrealistic Expectations:** Relying easily on a partner sets up expectations on how things should come out; but when results fail to meet expectations, bitterness sets in and a blaming game will be underway.
Division of Labor: Partners divide tasks fairly to ensure equal contributions to the business without being upset.	

Image-2: Partnership Pros & Cons vs. Solo Investing

After weighing up the upsides and downsides of entering into a partnership investing setup, as well as going solo (refer to Image-2), some investors opt to invest in real estate with a partner right from the very beginning. Others would rather choose to work alongside partners only on a deal-by-deal or case-by-case setup.

The bottom line of applying partnerships in real estate investing is having the assurance that both partners stay dedicated and committed to the business. Such certainty will most likely develop mutual success to all parties involved.

While several opinions abound about what business structure would be more appropriate to set up, when it would be high time to create one, and so forth, the business world regards *'incorporation'* as one of the ideal ways to protect you and your business from liabilities. An incorporated business entity structure has distinctive tax and legal identities separate from its owners.

In fact, the law considers a corporation as an individual. Hence, it can own property, pay taxes, earn income, incur liabilities, and even face legal suits.

Incorporating can offer numerous benefits to a business. Apart from limiting the liability of the shareholders for the company's debts, it has the ability to sell bonds or issue shares of stocks—both of which can raise added capital for the company. However, it is highly advisable to consult with your accountant or real estate attorney whenever you decide to incorporate your business.

To review, business plans and roadmaps are never hard and fast rules; but plainly, guides. It intends to lead you to the right direction, at the proper speed, and at a timely period while motivating you to carry it out through the end.

When putting your clearly defined plan into practice and envisioning its end, your goals become much more attainable. Although it may almost be impossible to follow a property investing or financial roadmap to a tee, you can always plot your course with extreme care and precision considering the several external forces at play.

"Buy real estate in areas where the path exists and buy more real estate where there is no path, but you can create your own."

—**David Waronker**, American Real Estate Investor

4-Real Estate Investment Market Niche Choices

"Before you start trying to work out which direction the real estate market is headed, you should be fully aware that there are markets within markets."

—**Paul Clitheroe**, Australian Financial Analyst

You might deem it at first to be important to know everything you can in the domain of real estate investing. Actually, it is just ideal to concentrate on a couple of aspects: choosing a type of investment vehicle and a methodical real estate strategy you will apply for your chosen investment vehicle.

This section introduces to you an outline of the most common investment options you can choose. With a diverse array of various property selections, real estate remains to be a preferred investment choice for many.

Its versatile field allows you sticking with either smaller traditional homes or much larger properties that can accommodate several tenants. Primarily, real estate enables you to own a property, for which you can have options of either renting it out to tenants or improving its conditions.

It can also give you the power to invest in either industrial or commercial properties. Generally, these types of properties involve certain business operations such as offices or retail shops that will be leasing the property from you. Sometimes, you might even simply fixate your mind on owning your dream property where you will live, together with your family.

Whatever investment plans you may have in mind, you will certainly find it much easier to invest into real estate and live with the potentials of earning a good deal of income along the process. In short, you will have endless possibilities with real estate investments while having the flexibility to adapt whenever you change your plans in the middle of your game.

However, after you have completed a full overview and review of all the different choices, only choose those investment vehicles that you feel most comfortable working with as an investor. You need not select all of them. Ideally, learning to invest successfully in real estate is simply choosing a single niche and striving hard towards mastering it.

Raw Lands

Raw land is plain and utter earth. It is a property without any infrastructures or structures. It has neither any improvements nor soil grading, nor site developments.

You can improve any piece of land to add its value. Cleaning it up, grading, and fencing the entire property can easily shoot up its price.

Initially, you will have the option of leasing out the bare land to create immediately your cash flow. You can also resurvey to subdivide the raw land and sell it for a profit.

Some real estate investors choose to purchase raw lands with the hopes that the property appreciates quickly someday. This sudden increase in the property value usually stems from external forces such as a construction of a major freeway or a nearby property development, or any establishments that create financial traffics.

Single-Family /Duplex/Triplex/Quads/Mobile Dwellings

For many first-time real estate investors, single-family housings are probably the most popular property investments of all. Typically, these properties are freestanding dwelling units, or detached houses, which do not share a wall with another house. However, these properties may also include townhouses, duplexes, triplexes, and quads or quadraplexes or fourplexes that all share a common wall.

It is noteworthy to know each of their precise terminologies for land zoning purposes, especially for loan programs that are only limited to single-family housings. In each instance though, your government's real estate laws, or those loan programs themselves, will be providing the proper definitions of the terms in accordance to their particular purposes.

Essentially, these properties are relatively easy to finance or qualify for a loan program, sell, and lease out. Each of them can serve either as a solid investment or as your personal residence. Nevertheless, it is obvious that income derived from the single-family rentals (SFRs) will not be able to provide you with a sufficient cash flow.

On the contrary, small multi-family properties (consisting of 2 to 4 housing units) combine entirely the benefits of a financing program and easy purchasing gains of a single-family dwelling. Banks usually weigh up these small multi-family properties with the same mortgage guidelines as a single-family housing unit.

Oftentimes, they have lesser competition than what you would expect when bidding on single-family homes. Statistics show that more people buy homes for residency than for business intents.

When bought properly, these properties can produce impressive cash flows. Additionally, they have the appealing faculty to take advantage of the *'economies-of-scale principle'*—or the reduction in unit cost resulting from more business or investment operations—since you only need a single loan program to secure those two, three, or four housing units in the entire property.

You can also begin investing in mobile housing units. Usually, this entails a lesser wherewithal out of your pocket since mobile homes cost lower per unit compared to single- and multi-family homes.

Another appealing quality of mobile home investing is that it commands a high demand in the market. Therefore, as a smart investor, you compel yourself to buy more of them with only less; along the process, you are actually spreading out the risks on your entire property investment portfolio.

Moreover, mobile housing properties usually have lesser tenant turnovers due to lower rentals. By these low vacancy rates, it only indicates that you will be incurring much lesser expenses for repairs, renovations, and maintenance on the property.

Small-or Large-Scale Apartments

Generally, real estate investors draw the line at 50 units when distinguishing between small-scale and large-scale apartment buildings. The former compose a minimum of five units while the latter starts comprising a minimum of 50 units.

Both properties are more difficult to finance than single- or multi-family housing properties. Fact is that they fall under commercial lending norms rather than residential loan programs.

A subset of large-scale apartments is the modern condominium. This property class refers to those huge and high advertising-budgeted residential cum commercial complexes, which usually include a gym, swimming pool, salons, diners, full-time staff, and security.

The cost of purchasing or financing or building these properties are extremely steep, but they can readily produce significant returns with only a minimal personal involvement. A partnership or *'syndication'*—an association of small investors or firms pooling their resources to carry out their enterprise—often owns and controls most of these large-scale apartments.

The basis for deriving the par value or minimum price for these properties usually comes from the total income they bring rather than being priced based on the *'appraised comparable properties'* or *'broker comparisons'* or simply, *'comps'*—statements brokers give to one another for confirming the price and size details of a transaction.

Therefore, this implies creating greater opportunities for increasing the value of the property by increasing its rentals, reducing expenditures, and managing it effectively. Regardless of scale, apartment buildings often provide stable and steady cash flows.

This is especially true for business-oriented investors who are very comfortable dealing with a much more intensive property management scheme. They can even utilize their property as their ideal office location for their on-site supervisors who will be managing and maintaining the property in exchange for discounted or free rentals.

In summary, the competition involved in this property investment niche is generally lower. On one hand, apartments are too small for those larger professional investment groups or real estate investment trusts (REITs) to invest. On the other hand, these properties are too large for many novice real estate investors.

Real Estate Investment Trusts (REITs)

Using the simplest comparison for its definitive term, a REIT is for real estate properties while a mutual fund is for stocks. Therefore, a REIT is an outfit that purchases real estate, particularly huge income-producing properties (i.e., large-scale apartment buildings, condominiums, warehouses, shopping complexes and malls, hotels, office skyscrapers, hospitals, timberlands or bulk quantities of single- or multi-family housing units).

It uses the funds pooled and invested by its shareholders as capital for its purchases. Thus, individual investors can acquire ownership in residential/commercial/industrial real estate portfolios. Shareowners receive individually prorated profits or dividends from the minimum 75% gross income of the REIT.

REITs involve one of the least hands-on approaches to real estate investing; yet, never expect their profit distributions to be similar to those returns manifested in intensively hands-on investment schemes. The numbers game or the total shareowners in a REIT (minimum of 100) play a big factor in your returns.

The hybrid REIT investments company also manages any realty loans incurred from its purchases. You can purchase shares in a REIT either directly on an open securities exchange or through investing in some mutual funds specializing in the public real estate or via your stock investments account if any.

Commercial Properties

Commercial real estate investments can vary impressively according to size, style, and usage or purpose (refer to Image-3).

Commercial Real Estate Category	Typical Examples
Healthcare	medical centers | clinics | hospitals | nursing homes
Industrial	industrial/factory buildings | distribution centers | garages or public parking lots | warehouses
Leisure	cafes | community centers | entertainment complexes | hotels | parks | public houses | restaurants | sports facilities
Office	professional office buildings | serviced offices | downtown skyscrapers | self-storage developments
Retail	pad sites on street frontages | 'power centers' with large anchor stores | retail shops | malls | single-tenancy retail buildings
Multi-Family Homes	multi-family housing units larger than fourplexes | high-rise apartment complexes

Image-3: Major Categories of Commercial Real Estate

Property investors classify only the first five categories as commercial income properties. Residential cum commercial properties can also denote multi-family apartments. Commercially zoned raw lands fall into commercial properties.

The bottom line of a commercial real estate ultimately involves buildings or land intended to generate a profit, from either capital gains or income derived from leasing to a business. Although they generally produce steady and substantive cash flows, commercial properties may sometimes bear prolonged holding periods. They sit idly and empty for several months or even years, especially during shifts of *'power centers'*—businesses that dominate their markets—as well as times of vacancies.

Therefore, lest you are beginning or coming from a very stable financial position, commercial real estate investing is an ill-advised investment route for you. Rather choose a real estate niche that has acquisition schemes commensurate with your schedules of finances.

Tax Lien Certificates

A tax lien takes place as a function of managing cash flow by the government (at either the municipal or federal state or national level). When property owners default on their quarterly property tax payments, the government imposes a tax lien on the property.

Hence, the government will have the right to foreclose or sell the property to other investors for a price equivalent to the taxes owed. Oftentimes, these tax lien sales connote to incredibly inexpensive properties.

Nevertheless, ensure doing your homework and exercising due diligence. Never jump straightaway into this type of real estate investing unprepared. Tax lien sales are usually complicated deals that require thorough research and experience.

You can purchase a *'tax lien certificate'*—a certified claim against a property with a government tax lien placed upon it due to unpaid property taxes—through an auction process. Normally, you pay downright the total delinquent property taxes owed before the redemption date.

The government, thereby, receives its cash immediately from the transaction. In return, you will have the right of collecting back your money, which includes penalty interest payments from the property owner.

The inclusive interest rates ensure tax liens certificates to be very attractive investments. Tax liens can promise returns of up to as high as 18% per annum (depending on the local jurisdiction of the property) with only minimal personal day-to-day management.

Mortgage Notes (Liens Landlordism)

Also known as a *'borrower's note,'* or a *'real estate lien note,'* a mortgage note is a promissory note secured by a specific mortgage firm upon an investor's acquisition of a property via a loan. Its contents explain the terms of the contract, declaring a promise of repayment of specified sums, including the specified interest rate, and the specified payment durations for fulfilling the promise.

Non-performing mortgage notes are primarily liens secured by real estate borrowers who have defaulted on their monthly obligations for various reasons. Usually, you can purchase these notes with significant discounts from willing private equity firms, hedge funds, and banks.

As a mortgage note buyer or investor, you will then have the right to start collecting the monthly loan payments. You will also have options of either keeping the note until the full payment of the mortgage or reselling it in the future. Like bonds, property mortgage notes can offer you a flow of payments over a certain period.

You can trade mortgage notes as part of a mortgage-backed security (MBS) or wholly on the *'secondary market,'* which refers to loans sold by a mortgage bank to some of the more popular government-sponsored enterprise (GSE) investors such as *'Fannie Mae'* and *'Freddie Mac.'*

Fannie Mae is actually the eponymous name of the *'Federal National Mortgage Association (FNMA),'* headquartered in the census-designated place (CDP) of Reston, Virginia, USA. Its brother GSE, Freddie Mac, also better known as the *'Federal Home Loan Mortgage Corporation (FHLMC),'* is also in the same locale.

Remember, when starting out, it would be prudent to narrow down choosing one, or at the most, a couple of real estate niches to put your focus on. Thereafter, work hard to become an expert in your chosen niche. Anyway, you can always expand mastering other niches later as you accumulate more in-depth knowledge and experiences in real estate investing.

"In the eyes of a real estate person, the most expensive part of the city is where one has a house to sell."

—**Will Rogers**, American Stage Actor &Humorist

5-Real Estate Investment Strategies: How to Build Long-Term Passive Wealth

"Do not wait to buy real estate; buy real estate and wait!"

—**T. Harv Eker**, American Motivational Speaker & Author

Prior to executing your actions on any of the aforementioned real estate market niches, bear a simplified understanding of how the cycle of the real estate market functions (refer to Image-4).

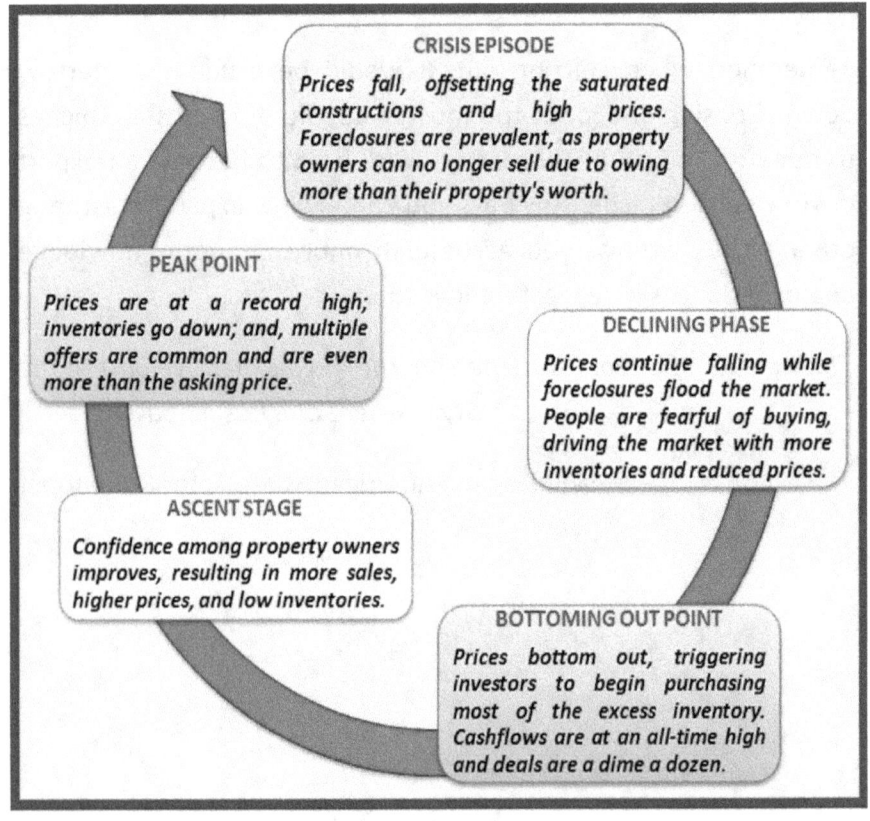

CRISIS EPISODE
Prices fall, offsetting the saturated constructions and high prices. Foreclosures are prevalent, as property owners can no longer sell due to owing more than their property's worth.

PEAK POINT
Prices are at a record high; inventories go down; and, multiple offers are common and are even more than the asking price.

DECLINING PHASE
Prices continue falling while foreclosures flood the market. People are fearful of buying, driving the market with more inventories and reduced prices.

ASCENT STAGE
Confidence among property owners improves, resulting in more sales, higher prices, and low inventories.

BOTTOMING OUT POINT
Prices bottom out, triggering investors to begin purchasing most of the excess inventory. Cashflows are at an all-time high and deals are a dime a dozen.

Image-4: Working Mechanisms of the Real Estate Market Cycle

In our modern times today, the necessity for land development becomes as constant as ever due to the world's increasing population growth, notwithstanding the changing discriminatory tastes and preferences of how people want to live. This perceived property demand creates the life cycle of the real estate market, which typically exists in all the real estate markets worldwide.

The real estate market cycle is a logical pattern of recurrent stages, which reflect the industry factors and forces such as fluctuating or falling prices; vacancies or rising inventories; and, lower inventories and skyrocketing prices due to high purchase and rental demands in the market. Simplistically, the cycle functions within and around two principal elements:

🏠 Firstly, a *'classical cycle of demand-and-supply'* occurs. This triggering phase determines property occupancies or vacancies that, in turn, define the rate of leasing or purchasing activities.

🏠 Secondly, an *'integrated financial cycle'* follows; whereby, the flows of capital (usually derived from the government's economic regulations) influence directly the market prices.

Similar to economic or business cycles, the property cycle typically goes full circle within at least a span of a decade. As economic conditions influence considerably entire markets, each stage of the real estate cycle poses as global forces that greatly affect the different sectors of society...and YOU, as a real estate investor!

Therefore, it is important to keep a comprehensive analysis of the nature of your chosen real estate market niche vis-à-vis the causes and effects of the economic atmosphere that currently prevails. Your sensible evaluations and projections will direct you towards the most logical step to make or strategy to implement.

Henceforth, as you begin to take actions on your chosen real estate market niche, it is always necessary to learn to interpret the market conditions, forces, and cycles. More importantly, master the essential real estate strategies, which you will apply for your chosen niche. These following basic property investment techniques will enable you to build and earn steadily long-term passive wealth.

Buy-and-Hold

The buy-and-hold real estate investment strategy is probably the purest, simplest, and most common way of real estate investing. It primarily ignores both short- and medium-term modes; rather, it focuses exclusively on a longer-term trend.

Essentially, real estate investors practicing this strategy seek to create long-term passive income by purchasing a piece of real estate and renting it out for an indefinitely extended period. Either the investors collect the property's monthly cash flow or simply hold the property out until such time in the future when they deem proper to let go of it for greater financial gains.

In this case, you need not do any trading activities on your investment portfolio between the time of acquiring a property and the end of the holding period (which is typically a longer duration). Especially during difficult times of temporary downturns in economic activities, the buy-and-hold strategy actually sways you to do away of any further negotiations (usually based on emotions), which you might enter or execute foolishly.

Generally, the technique yields solid returns as the market projects perceived upward trends over time. Nevertheless, the buy-and-hold method can be remarkably risky.

In particular, the value of your property can fall to as much as 20%, or even more amidst prolonged periods of a severe *'bear market'*—a market situation wherein prices show declining trends. A bear market is the opposite of a *'bull market,'* whereby, the market exhibits rising prices, which tend to frustrate smaller investors to acquire properties.

A dominant advantage of the buy-and-hold strategy is that it offers to increase your equity or value in the property. The appreciation comes from decreasing your principal mortgage balance as you keep paying it down throughout the entire period you are holding and renting out the property.

For a buy-and-hold investor, it is most important to understand how to assess the market for opportunities and evaluate deals. The usual misstep new investors commit while using this strategy is purchasing unfavorable deals since they simply do not have a good grasp of property and market evaluations.

Other usual issues include the underestimation of expenditures and cash flow disbursements, execution of poor decisions, and the failure of managing the property effectively. You can avoid all these mistakes if you will only learn how to identify properly the characteristics of the property market, its ebbs and flows or fluctuations, and the prevailing stage of its cycle (review Image-2).

When you ultimately perceive that the property market or the real estate niche you desire seems to glide down towards a declining phase and a bottoming out period (high inventories and low prices), it would simply be ideal to seek out and purchase your preferred real estate. Capitalize on the situation; strike while the market is hot!

Conversely, when you assess that the market accelerates until being *'overheated'* (tending towards inflation due to excessive growth demands), the usual route to take is to cease purchasing until a normalcy settles back down. During these stages in the market cycle, you may either sell or merely continue holding over your properties.

Some buy-and-hold investors would never sell a property; instead, they choose to undertake a strategic style of *'passive management'*—the investing strategy of waiting it out while tracking market movements and indications. They just pay off their mortgage balances to create more equity while subsisting on the cash flow of their properties held.

Others may ultimately find it timely to sell their holdover properties by applying *'seller-financing'*—a property selling procedure on which you fund the purchase to the buyer through your loan; the buyer only takes the title of the property when fully repaying the loan (refer further to Section-9 for your investment exit strategies).

Flipping

The real estate investment strategy of flipping is easily the most popular, especially in the U.S. Its popularity (or notoriety?) is due to its firm impressions on pop culture, which also promotes it (i.e., "Flip This House" TV series). Investors mostly use the term to describe purely a *'residential redevelopment'* or renovation.

Somehow, redevelopment of distressed properties or abandoned neighborhoods sometimes connotes to unscrupulous and malicious acts during post-housing bubble periods. Thus, flipping oftentimes denotes as both a derogatory and a descriptive term.

On one hand, its socially destructive and illegal schemes involve *'market manipulation'*—a deliberate attempt at interfering with the free and fair real estate market operations. Usually, the interference is the deceptive creation of false, artificial, or misleading appearances with respect to property prices or values, or even the entire market itself.

In the United Kingdom, the term depicts an unethical technique used by Members of Parliament for switching their second homes between several other houses. The effects enable them to maximize their allowances funded by taxpayers' money!

In its pure essence, flipping is the real estate investing practice of purchasing a revenue-generating piece of real estate at a typically discounted or moderate price; and thereafter, improving the property in certain ways (i.e., redevelopment, renovation, remodeling, etc.), and ultimately, reselling it for a profit in the shortest time possible.

The schematic description of real estate flipping is relatively similar to the retail business style of *'purchasing low and selling high.'* Flipping techniques can function in a couple of acquisition models:

🏠 **Multi-Purchase**: You may buy several properties with the intent of selling them within a short time, hoping that market prices go up. This flipping model would be ideal in areas with a promising future of undergoing large-scale developments.

🏠 **Single-Purchase:** You may buy a solitary property that has already some obvious improvements. You can then tweak some minor renovations on it, with the purpose of selling it for a much greater price than its initial cost.

Generally, flipping applies more notably to investing in single-family housing units. Guided by the 70%-acquisition principle, a knowledgeable house flipper will purchase a single housing unit worth 70% of its prevailing value less any rehabilitation costs.

For instance, a housing unit should have a value of $150,000 if it was in mint condition or in tiptop shape; yet, it necessitates $30,000 worth of rehab works. An experienced flipper will buy the property for only half its value, or $75,000 (that is, 70% of $150,000 less $30,000). Subsequently, the flipper seeks to sell the completely redeveloped property for the full $150,000!

Speed is one essential key aspect in flipping. Flippers follow a streamlined procedure of buying, redeveloping, and selling real estate as quickly as possible.

The speedy rate ensures optimum profitability while avoiding long durations of higher *'carrying costs'*—expenses of unproductive assets incurred by ownership, which usually include monthly bills such as utilities, property taxes, financing charges, and other maintenance fees necessary in retaining the positive financial standing of the property.

By its nature, which involves redevelopment works, flipping is typically an *'active management'* style of investing. Additionally, its management has the basic premise of maximizing investment returns by executing the flipping procedures on a regular basis.

Therefore, as you stop flipping, you actually cease earning money until you start flipping again. Several investors opt to apply flipping so they could fund their routine bills, including the provision of the wherewithal for other additional passive property investments.

Wholesaling | Contract Assignment

The real estate strategy of wholesaling is the process of looking for promising real estate deals, signing a contract and placing a measly deposit (usually, as little as $10) for acquiring the deal, and then, entering into another contract with a third party buyer for reselling the same property at a much higher price. The third party buyer receives all the rights to the initial purchase contract and pays the wholesaler an *'assignment fee'* (usually ranging from $500 to $5,000 or higher, depending on the deal).

Usually, the original purchase contract stipulates for an *'inspection period.'* The original buyer (wholesaler) exploits this stipulating clause to gain time looking for a third party buyer and assigning the contract. When there are no buyers available, this leeway period allows the wholesaler to withdraw from the contract and get back the deposit.

In most cases, wholesalers never intend to purchase and own the piece of property. Instead, they simply apply the wholesaling technique as an instrument to search promising properties for other real estate investors or retail buyers. Oftentimes, they sell their contracts to typical cash buyers like house flippers, who pay them within just a short time.

Thus, a wholesaler is essentially an intermediary paid for finding deals. As such, wholesalers do not have any obligations on renovation works and costs, building contractors, mortgage fees, banking transactions, tenancy agreements, or other similar complications. It is no wonder why several investors opt to start with wholesaling because it primarily features simple and easy procedures with low startup costs.

In a successful wholesaling transaction, the seller is often not aware that the original buyer does not intend to purchase the property. In other cases, however, wholesalers actually purchase the property in cold cash, and then, they resell the property in a second closing to their end buyer.

Such wholesaling practice may be more costly because these wholesalers pay the closing costs of the purchase and resell the property. Nevertheless, *'double closing,'* or paying two closing costs, often makes sense (apart from being more ethical) for wholesalers, especially with deals projecting substantial profits from reselling. Besides, double closing transactions prevent requests of large assignment fees.

Furthermore, *'multiple wholesaling,'* or reassigning real estate purchase contracts multiple times from the original wholesaler to the end buyer, is a common moneymaking transaction for a number of wholesalers. In several cases, fellow wholesalers collaborate to ensure that all parties involved earn favorably on the entire transaction.

The real estate community perceives this conspiratorial practice of wholesaling to be illegal or unethical. Yet, in principle and in practice, nothing is actually illegal in assigning multiple rights to a property purchase contract. In the first place, the contract tolerates it.

Truth is that property wholesaling is no different from the wholesaling nature in other fields. It is also worth knowing that the basic reason for such an opportunity to wholesale is the fact that the original owner intends selling the property for considerably less than its fair market value.

This usually happens when either the original seller or the property is in distress. Perhaps, the property has undergone severe damages from a storm, flood, or fire; or, the original seller is on the brink of losing the property due to foreclosure.

Originally, the real estate industry termed the practice of buying properties way below their market value as, *'distressed real estate investing.'* Due to the substantially low prices and high probabilities of a quantity surge of distressed properties, the term evolved into *'wholesale real estate investing;'* thus, the coinage of its practitioner as, *'wholesaler.'*

As a wholesaler, you should seek out continuously the rosy deals to build up an ample inventory to sell. Using a variety of real estate marketing strategies can help you to realize the best finds.

Additionally, seek out continuously the right buyers for the deals you acquire. Cash buyers can help you to grow your solid network of connections in the real estate community.

Although promoted as a strategy that someone with no money or anyone can perform, wholesaling ultimately requires you to grow your financial resources so you can design and develop your marketing funnel. Persist to persevere in enhancing your wholesaling skills.

"Buy on the fringe and wait. Buy land near a growing city! Buy real estate when other people want to sell. Hold what you buy!"

—**John Jacob Astor IV**, American Real Estate Builder & Investor

6-Acquiring & Purchasing of Real Estate Investments

"Working-class neighborhoods have the best and highest yielding properties to invest; all fancy properties are overpriced."

—**Jane Bryant Quinn**, American Financial Journalist

At this point, you may now have completed training your focus on the necessary preparations prior to investing. Nevertheless, it is never enough to analyze a deal. In the fullness of time, you will need to dive deep down and purchase your first real estate.

Since it would be your primary purchase, ensure that it must also be a PRIME endeavor! The following topics will dwell on the prime ways to help you to search for the best property deal, negotiate for its acquisition, make your profit from it, and ensure you arrive at the closing stage and complete it in one piece.

Foremost, bear in mind that in property investing, *'you should always create your profit when you acquire or purchase a piece of real estate.'* In most instances, you do not begin your property-investing career simply by bagging a big fat check. Such windfalls only take place after you have implemented completely and successfully your investment strategies and plans.

At the time of the acquisition, you can either realize or destroy the profits you create. To create your profit when purchasing, you must buy a deal pegged at a price that will assure you of achieving your most coveted profits based on your capability of executing your exit (or selling) strategy. In short, you just simply ought to BUY SMARTLY.

If you have overpaid stupendously for a piece of property, then it would be a prime failure of investing! No matter how you hope and wish for any occurrences of appreciations or improvements in the market, the purchase will never be a worthwhile investment.

You can never predict precisely the future movements in the market, or know where it is exactly heading to go; however, you can always know its current situation. Hence, always be discerning about the fair market value appraisal of a piece of real estate.

The appraised *'fair market value (FMV)'* of a property is its subjective estimated price for which a willing buyer would pay a willing seller, assuming both have a fair knowledge of the property's facts and worth. To determine an asset's FMV, your wisest method is to compare the prices others have paid for something comparable.

Property Investment Shopping Parameters

As you have already known the importance of locking down or arranging to secure your profits right from the start of acquiring a prime property, do not be in a rush to begin searching for the best deal. You must also understand that the exciting field of real estate can overwhelm you with its array of different niches, as well as strategies. You will be prone to getting distractions by its next big craze or the enormous volumes of deals in the market.

Hence, before starting your search, you must first focus on defining your property investment selection parameters. By defining your shopping criteria, it enables you to narrow down your purchasing options in the market. Primarily, you will eliminate an extensive list of irrelevant deals that chiefly serve as distractions, if not, a waste of time in your searching process.

Instead, you will exclusively have a clear look for those right kinds of properties that you are most interested in acquiring. Not only will your structured parameters help you to avoid falling into a state of analysis paralysis but also, they will enable you to stay on track towards acquiring your prime property investment deal.

Imagine your selection criteria as your grocery list. It will keep you focused on shopping only for the items you need without wasting your money and time on other attractive items along the aisle.

Then again, your list of property shopping parameters should primarily be a clear derivation of your chosen type of property niche to invest in and the property investing strategy you opt to apply. With these fundamental derivatives in mind, you can then structure your selection list with the necessary measures to include. Generally, the most significant items or property factors you might want to consider adding to your list are the following:

🏠 **Appreciation Potential**

🏠 **Cash Flow Production (Rental or Selling Ability)**

🏠 **Community or Neighborhood (Accessibility to Amenities)**

🏠 **Locality (Inclusive Real Estate Laws)**

🏠 **Property Conditions**

🏠 **Quantity of Units**

🏠 **Size of the Property (Floor Space, Total Lot Size, Terrain)**

🏠 **Type of Zoned Property (Raw Land, Residential, Commercial)**

🏠 **Capitalization Rate**

'Capitalization rate,' or cap rate for short, is the net income a property produces within a given year divided by its purchase price, expressed in percentage. Apparently, this is your basic real estate valuation parameter that you must use to compare different property investments.

Cap rates help you to determine the property's *'rate of return,'*—how fast a property pays for itself, and thereby, begins making a profit. For instance, if a property costs $500,000 and it nets an income of $50,000 in a year, the cap rate is 10%. Thus, it will take 10 years to pay for the property with the proceeds it produces.

Nobody can dictate exactly to you what your investment property criteria must include or not. All the items on your list boil down to your personal choices, just as your preferred niche and strategy.

Therefore, your chosen criteria will be revolving around the type of investment you wish to engage. For instance, if you wish to engage in 'buy-and-hold investing' of smaller multi-family housing units, your shopping parameter must include such type of buildings and exclude commercial properties.

Understanding Financial Rules of Property Investing

The financial aspects (i.e., cash flow production, appreciation potential, capitalization rate, etc.) of real estate investing are explicitly the most important components in your property shopping parameter list. In the first place, you cannot create your profit from the property of you put these financial aspects aside.

In other words, a property deal that does not bear a coherently financial sense is never going to be a solid investment for you. Thus, the issue is to know the financial information of the deal.

However, a property listing does not generally present any financial information about a deal. Although you can determine easily how much income the property produces, you would not know immediately the precise amounts of monthly cash flow the property makes or how much overpriced the entire deal is.

Just the same, you do not exactly know what you should offer on the table. It does not even help to form your offer if you get your spreadsheet out and perform a thorough evaluation of a property on every single deal you consider. Besides, it is not sensible.

During these circumstances, the financial rules of property investment gush forth. These following rules will serve as your guide for rendering quickly on the fly certain evaluations on the financial aspect of a property; hence, they help you to decide whether the deal warrants a further look and consideration:

❖ The 2%-Rental Rule

This rule enables you to evaluate the potential cash flow production of a property. It declares that the rental should be about 2% of the selling price. Hence, for a $50,000-property, the monthly rent should be $1,000.

In most places, applying the 2%-rental rule could be tough to achieve. However, the closer you are able to reach it, the higher will be your chances of gaining a better cash flow.

Actual Application Example: In a certain community, a 3-bedroom medium-sized housing unit has a prevailing rental rate of $600 per month. By applying the 2%-rental rule, you should be expecting to spend about $30,000 for the acquisition of such a property (that is, $600 ÷ 2% = $30,000).

❖ The 50%-Expenditure Rule

This rule enables you to predict accurately the monthly expenses that you will incur for a certain property. It declares that 50% of the property's monthly income will be your operating expenses, which exclude mortgage payments.

Most property listings will only inform you about the monthly income of a listed property. When dividing the property income in half, the quotient gives you an idea of how much money you will have left for paying its monthly mortgage.

Therefore, your cash flow is equivalent to whatever income left after deducting all the expenses and mortgage payment. Usually, the 50%-expenditures may include taxes, insurance, repairs, utilities, vacancies, turnover costs, management, and the reserved *'capital expenses (CapEx),'* earmarked for the sporadic big-ticket repair items like a garage, heating/cooling systems, roofing, etc.

Actual Application Example: A 10-door medium-rise apartment building produces a monthly income of $10,000. By applying the 50%-expenditure rule, you will have $5,000 left to pay for the mortgage. If you pay a monthly mortgage fee of $3,000, then you can anticipate reasonably a cash flow of $2,000 per month.

❖ The 70%-ARV Pricing Rule

This rule enables you to determine quickly the maximum future selling price you should be paying for a property based on its appraised *'after repair value (ARV)'*—an estimated future value (not a current value) for a distressed property after conducting and completing its repair/rehab works. It declares that you must only pay 70% of the ARV appraisal minus the rehab expenses.

70

Therefore, the ARV includes both the value of the renovations on a property and its purchase price. Fix-and-flip investors commonly apply this rule. However, you can also apply it to any investment strategies when finding a good deal.

Actual Application Example: A residential property sells approximately for $300,000 after you will have renovated or fixed it up. As you may estimate, you need about $30,000 worth of repair works. By applying the 70%-ARV rule, you arrive at multiplying 70% by $300,000 to get the product of $210,000 for which you will deduct the repair cost of $30,000 from it. Hence, the maximum price you should only be paying for the property is $180,000 while having a future profit of $120,000.

Remember that you will only use these financial rules for deciding whether a property is worth examining further for its suitability and profitability; or, screening it out downright and efficiently. Never use these rules to decide exactly the amount you will be paying for a property; or, whether you should invest in it or not.

All these rules simply provide you with conservative estimates. However, if a property passes or gets close to the estimates of any of the rules, then you may endorse the examined property for more detailed analyses on your spreadsheet. Do not interpret these rules for a license to omitting your homework.

Finding the Ideal Real Estate Investment Deals

If you have already completed your property shopping parameter list, then you are all set to start finding for your best investment property deals. Of course, those ubiquitous ad signs at the forefronts of houses for sale are a given; yet, you will have several other ways to search for your investment properties.

Some properties might have concealed issues you need to resolve. Others might just simply require you to inspect them so you can easily figure out how much are their real worth. You can even acquire properties through auctions or work with foreclosed pieces of real estate. Explore further the following different channels where you can exploit to the hilt to look for your deals:

Word-of-Mouth: Some property owners still stick to the old-fashioned way of selling via word-of-mouth. You can be in the best position to search for your property deals when you inform everyone within and outside your circles about your presence and intentions of buying in the market. You may also inform directly your peers or the members of your locality's real estate club.

The Multiple Listing Service (MLS): The MLS is a suite of services commonly used by real estate brokers—representing either buyers or sellers—to establish unilateral contractual compensation offers among fellow brokers and disseminate the information to enable price comparisons (brokers comparison) and appraisals. Its database has a vast collection of property deals for sale all over the country. You are actually searching the MLS when you are searching full-service property brokerage sites such as redfin.com or realtor.com.

Outbound Marketing: Going out with sellers can be more than helpful and productive in your property search since it often involves advertising, direct mail, and other marketing modes.

LoopNet.com: It is the world's largest and most heavily trafficked online marketplace for publicly listed commercial real estate for lease or sale—from small multi-family units to large-scale apartment buildings, shopping complexes, restaurants, etc.

🏠 **Craigslist.org:** Being in the world's top 50 most popular websites, the free online classified ads portal is where millions of people prefer to buy, sell, and trade almost any item one can think of, including all types of real estate.

🏠 **National/Local Dailies:** Although the major dailies are fading quickly from circulation, many realtors still place their listings in the classified ads section of national newspapers or your local dailies. These channels are some of the bright places to scour for properties that are usually for-sale-by-owner.

Property Purchasing Process: 'From Offer to the Keys'

Acquiring or purchasing real estate does not simply involve writing the check for the offer and getting the keys to the property. The buying and selling of real estate is actually a complex process.

Oftentimes, the property purchasing process is a long and arduous effort that composes of several dynamic stages. Learn the following stages as you walk through the entire procedural process—from offer to the keys:

Stage One – Decide to choose on your property market niche and investing strategy (refer back to Section 4 and Section 5).

Stage Two – Define clearly your property selection parameters.

Stage Three – Decide to choose on your financing mode for the deal (refer to Section 7). This implies that you have a definite plan on how you will purchase the property. Whichever financial vehicle you will use, ensure that you are ready for their requisites (i.e., liquid cash to dispose of, pre-approval for a bank loan, etc.).

Stage Four – Start searching for your desired property deal at all possible avenues, as aforementioned in this section. Perhaps, you might contact a real estate agent at this stage since their services are generally free of charge for buyers. (Typically, brokers receive compensation from the closing costs of the seller.)

However, you can also forego the services of a broker, and rather contact the sellers themselves. This would be ideal if you are directly dealing with properties not listed on the MLS.

Stage Five – Filter out the deals through your list of selection parameters so you can screen out quickly the duds.

Stage Six – Do your homework and execute due diligence. Inspect thoroughly all the details and conditions of the property.

Stage Seven – Make an offer on the deal/s, which you desire to pursue. You may either offer your minimum or maximum purchasing limits or offer much less than the amount you are willing to spend. Typically, you make an offer inclusive with a contract—the purchase and sale agreement—for which your broker will be doing it for you.

If you are not using the services of a broker, or you are not purchasing a property listed in the MLS, then you can actually avail for a purchase and sale agreement template online or at an office supply store. You can also get it free from a title and escrow servicing company or through your real estate attorney, which is highly advisable for a careful review of the terms.

Step Eight – Negotiate the deal and your offer with the seller. Always, have the intent of mutually coming to terms with the price and the stipulations of the agreement.

Stage Nine – Submit the property details and all its pertinent documents to either your attorney or a title and escrow company (depending on your location; other areas do not use the services of a title and escrow outfit) for the initial process of docketing and transferring the ownership of title to your name.

At this stage, you will also comply with the required paperwork for your financing, hire contractors (if redevelopment works are necessary), confirm the validity of the financial aspects or profitability of the property, and prepare to handle any untoward issues that may arise during the closing.

This entire stage can take you from several days to months or even more to accomplish, depending on the situation. Generally, the process takes longer with bank financing. Hence, closings are much quicker when using an all-cash purchase.

Stage Ten – Sign the documents with your attorney or the title and escrow company. After the docketing or recording process of the paperwork, you officially become the new owner of the property!

"Buying real estate is not only the best way, the quickest way, the safest way, but the only way to become wealthy."

—**Marshall Field**, American Entrepreneur & Retailer

7-Applying Real Estate Financing Vehicles

"Do not stretch yourself too much with a mortgage. Buy within your means...it is not worth the sleepless nights."

—Sarah Beeny

There is no such thing as free real estate unless you inherit it from your folks. Just like any other commodity, you have to pay—in any way—for any kind real estate if you want to acquire it.

As a property investor, one of your most significant abilities to master is to look for creative ways to move continuously forward with your investments. Since no deals are exactly similar to one another, you would be structuring eventually each of your deals by choosing and using a mode of financing from a variety of real estate financing tools.

Therefore, it is important to have a thorough understanding of the different financing strategies, which will help you to earn more income and progress throughout your property-investing career. Fact is that these financing options are your lifelines; they are the indispensable vehicles you will ride towards reaching your destination of real estate investing success.

Nevertheless, beware of the advantages that financing offers. Financing is convenient and gives you a relief; but somehow, it may manifest at a much bigger cost. Essentially, you commit a substantive portion of your future income in order to obtain utility at the present for the costs of accrued interest spread across several years. Know and watch out for the hidden hazards.

Learning how to handle loans or mortgages of this nature enables you to benefit optimally from them. Yet, if you ignore the risks involved, it can lead you to major pitfalls.

Hereunder is the following list of the most common financing methods used by property investors. Albeit not comprehensive, it gives you an overview to help you devise a potent combination of real estate investment strategies—a specific property market niche, a property investing scheme, and a financing instrument to manage any real estate investment.

All-Cash Purchase

Many property investors opt to pay 100% of their investment with cold cash, which is money readily at hand for disposal. They pay in this method for varying reasons (i.e., to avoid high-interest financing rates, to achieve a faster and smoother closing, etc.).

For clarity, although investors commonly use the term, 'all-cash,' for such a purchase option, the reality is that cold cash is absent and never traded in the transaction. Generally, all-cash buyers pay by using a check. However, a property seller typically requires from an all-cash buyer a guarantee that the check payment will surely satisfy the obligated selling price.

In most cases, the all-cash investor brings to a title/escrow company a check, which is usually in the form of *'certified funds,'*—a form of payment guaranteed to settle, and issued by a company (bank) certifying the funds (i.e., a manager's check, bank cashier's check or known as bank draft in Canada, money order, etc.). The title/escrow company will then write the check to the seller. Other times, the all-cash investor consummates the payment via wire transfer or electronic bank transfer (EBT).

The all-cash purchase option is the easiest method of financing your investment since it has typically no inclusive complications. Nevertheless, for the vast majority of new property investors, an all-cash payment is not an option. The returns from an all-cash transaction are never the same as when leveraged.

Actual Application Example: You have $200,000 to invest. On one hand, you can choose to use your available cash to purchase a property that will produce for you a monthly income of $2,000, or $24,000 per year. This translates to a 20% ROI.

On the other hand, you could also rather use your $200,000 as a 20%-down payment for five similar properties, each listed at $200,000. Hence, the mortgage on each property will be $160,000 while having an approximated cash flow of $1,500 per month for each property. This equates to a monthly income of $7,500, or $90,000 per year; thus, translating to a whopping 45% ROI, which is more than twice better than purchasing just a single property!

Cash-Down Payment + Mortgage Application

As you can figure out from the aforementioned example, acquiring your property through mortgage financing can give you a significantly better ROI compared to an all-cash purchase. It is no wonder why most property investors—even if they have the required full cash payment—would rather choose to finance their investment properties with a cash-down payment plus a conventional mortgage application.

Investors commonly use a conventional mortgage because of its relatively low-interest rates. Generally, conventional mortgages require only a minimum down payment of 20%; but, depending on the lender, they can extend to 25% to 30% for properties.

You can apply for a conventional mortgage loan from a wide variety of lending sources (i.e., mortgage brokers, banks, and credit unions). Oftentimes, most of these financing institutions do not actually use their own resources for funding your loan.

Instead, they either borrow the funding capital from another party or resell your loan to government-sponsored enterprises (GSEs) such as Fannie Mae or Freddie Mac so they could replenish their own finances. In effect, these lending institutions adhere to rigorous standards and stringent guidelines in terms of investment financing that can be tough for investors to obtain.

Nevertheless, some financing institutions have the ability to be *'portfolio lenders'*—lending sources that use entirely their own portfolio of funds to lend to borrowers instead of selling the applied loan. Since the funds are their own, they can provide borrowers with more flexible qualifying standards and loan terms.

Most of these portfolio lenders never advertise being one, but you can find them through networking with other investors or referrals from your peers. You may also simply grab a directory, call each of them, and ask whether they offer portfolio lending.

Federal Housing Administration (FHA) & 203K Loans

The Federal Housing Administration (FHA) is a government-supported program that works as an insurer of loans or mortgages for banking institutions. Its working concept is similar to the operations of your car or health insurance.

It pools financial resources to spread the risk across for everyone. The program's design is to offer loans only for homeowners who are going to live in the property.

Therefore, you cannot avail for an FHA-supported loan to purchase a property intended purely for investment. However, its rule has an exception for which you can exploit.

It allows the FHA-financed property to have a maximum of four separate units. Hence, if you plan to reside in one unit, you could purchase a duplex, triplex, or quadraplex.

The beauty of an FHA loan requires applicants a very low down payment, which is at 3.5% as of 2018. This advantageous requirement can certainly help you to get moving much sooner because you no longer need to save up for more just as you would in meeting the usual 20%-down payment imposed by conventional mortgages.

Nevertheless, an FHA loan is not entirely a sweet deal. When purchasing a property with a down payment of less than 20%, the FHA requires you to buy a *'private mortgage insurance (PMI),'* which protects the FHA against the risk of defaulting on your loan.

Expected PMI premiums you will pay vary, but they are typically at 0.5% of the total amount loaned. Some borrowers avoid the PMI by taking out a *'piggyback mortgage,'* which is actually a second mortgage that allows them to borrow up to 100% of the property's value; whereby, the loan-to-value ratio in the primary mortgage is around 80% while the piggyback has 20%.

A subset of the FHA loan is the *'203K loan.'* This type of loan allows homeowners to purchase a housing unit that requires some rehabilitation works while providing them with the ability to finance the redevelopments into the loan itself. Similar to the regular FHA loan, the 203K loan facility requires a low down payment requirement stipulated by the FHA at 3.5%.

Actual Application Example: *You found a duplex for $140,000 that you desire moving into, with plans of residing in one unit while renting out the other. As per your estimates, the property requires about $10,000 for renovation works. You were able to incorporate the renovation cost into your initial loan amount, aggregating the loan to $150,000. For a 3.5%-down payment on your total loan, you paid $5,250.*

You can now start your renovation works (paid for by your loan), fulfill moving into your renovated unit while renting out the other, and start creating your cash flow and growing your wealth.

A 203K loan also follows the same FHA guidelines, stating that the occupant of the housing unit must be the homeowner-borrower. Likewise, the loan is applicable for acquiring duplexes, triplexes, and quadraplexes, as well as requiring a PMI for loans below 20%.

HomePath | Fannie Mae | Freddie Mac Mortgages

The HomePath property mortgage program is another GSE loan facility launched by Fannie Mae, the mortgage giant owned by the government. Its introduction to the real estate industry attempts to revive their ***'non-performing loans,'*** or foreclosed properties, into profitable loans on the ***'secondary mortgage market.'***

The HomePath, as the FHA has, also allows for a relatively small down payment, pegged at 10% as of 2018. However, it does not require any mortgage insurance like a PMI.

The loan is applicable for property investors who do not necessarily have to occupy their loaned property. It also includes the ability to integrate financing renovation works into the purchase loan similar to the 203K loan.

Just as you would likely deem a HomePath loan to be a bed of roses, it has its own caveat. The availability of all loans it offers is only on bank repossessions owned exclusively by Fannie Mae.

Hence, HomePath is only the brand used for all properties owned by Fannie Mae. Fannie Mae controls everything behind the scenes. It collaborates with housing counselors or real estate attorneys, partners, and other mortgage service providers to help and encourage homeowners to avoid foreclosure.

With Freddie Mac, property investors can earn extra financing by trading mortgage notes. Freddie Mac fundamentally operates by charging a guarantee fee on property mortgages it purchases on the *'secondary mortgage market'*—also known as the *'follow-on public offering'* or *'aftermarket.'*

With these purchases, the secondary mortgage market expands its flows of money. This increased financial supply becomes available for lending to investors, as well as for new homebuyers. In effect, you can also secure loans from these markets.

Freddie Mac gathers all its purchased loans together and trades or sells them to investors as securitized bonds or *'mortgage-backed securities (MBS)'* on the open market. Investors receive part of the interest and principal payments on the traded mortgage notes.

However, these investors/purchasers of Freddie Mac-MBS are more than willing to give back the fees to Freddie Mac in exchange for the guaranteed assumption of Freddie Mac on the credit risk, regardless if the borrower actually repays or not. Thus, MBS are exceptionally attractive to investors due to the financial guarantee of Freddie Mac.

Property Owner-Financing Scheme

Giant lending institutions or other traditional lending entities are not the only sources that can help to finance your property acquisition. In some cases, the property owner for whom you want to purchase real estate can actually fund your purchase.

In this case, you will simply send your monthly payments directly to the property owner. Actually, the only event property owners will offer such financing mode is when they already have absolute ownership of the home.

This means that the property owner/seller is clear and free from any mortgage on the concerned property. If the seller has an existing loan and sells the property to you, the seller must pay the loan immediately lest facing foreclosure.

This compulsory full payment stems from the legal provision stipulated on almost all loan agreements—the *'due-on-sale clause.'* This empowers the lender to cite the mortgage note as *'due immediately.'* If unpaid, the lender forecloses the property.

Of course, you may also assume wholly the current property loan of the seller and work out a favorable deal for all parties. The industry calls this tactical scheme as *'carrying-the-contract,'* which can also be a strategic instrument to apply when you decide to sell your properties in the future.

If all the conditions are proper and run smoothly, the property owner-financing scheme is truly a great and convenient mode to acquire ownership of a piece of real estate. You will no longer need to avail the financing services of a bank or other financial institutions.

Hard Money & Private Money Financing

Hard money financing is a quick loan you can readily obtain from a private individual or business for the sole purpose of residential real estate investing. It is similar to a *'bridge loan,'* which refers exclusively to commercial property investments. Although both of its underlying styles and terms can vary every now and then, the hard money financing method has the following defining features:

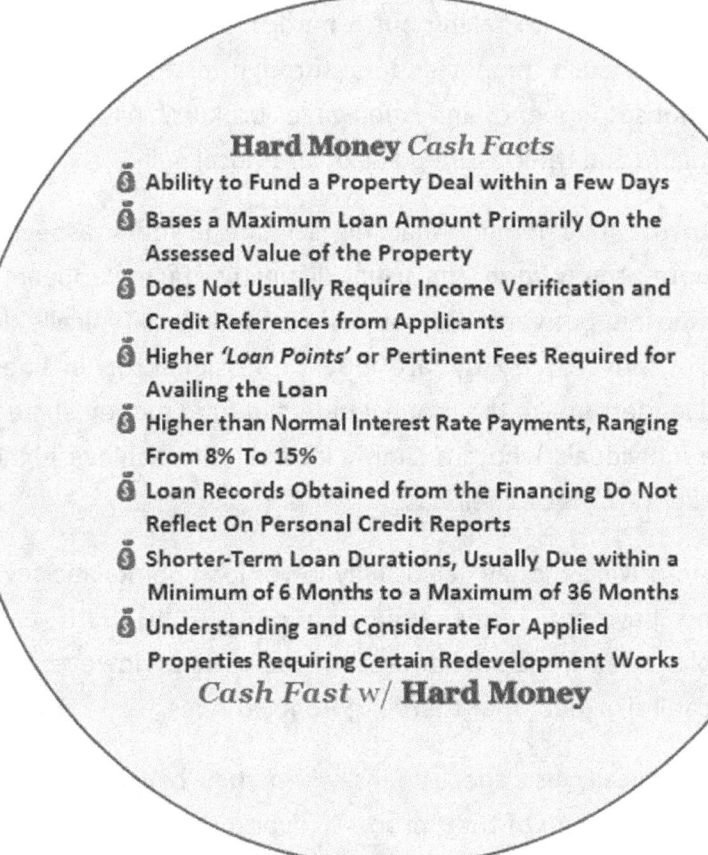

Hard Money *Cash Facts*

- Ability to Fund a Property Deal within a Few Days
- Bases a Maximum Loan Amount Primarily On the Assessed Value of the Property
- Does Not Usually Require Income Verification and Credit References from Applicants
- Higher *'Loan Points'* or Pertinent Fees Required for Availing the Loan
- Higher than Normal Interest Rate Payments, Ranging From 8% To 15%
- Loan Records Obtained from the Financing Do Not Reflect On Personal Credit Reports
- Shorter-Term Loan Durations, Usually Due within a Minimum of 6 Months to a Maximum of 36 Months
- Understanding and Considerate For Applied Properties Requiring Certain Redevelopment Works

Cash Fast w/ **Hard Money**

Image-5: Defining Characteristics of a Hard Money Financing Scheme

Mostly, a hard money loan is expedient for situations that demand immediate funding, which is synonymous with distressed financial situations (i.e., arrears on the existing mortgage, occurring bankruptcy and foreclosure). Applied almost exclusively in the U.S. and Canada, it has developed into the last resort for property owners due to its excessively higher interest rates.

85

Hence, use this loan with caution. Ensure having in place multiple exit strategies prior to taking out a hard money loan. Generally, you can find such moneylenders through asking real estate agents, house flippers, and mortgage brokers, or search at craigslist.com and the classified ads of your local daily.

Similar to the hard money-financing scheme in many aspects is the *'private money loan.'* Its usual distinctive factor appears in the relationship between the borrower and lender. Typically, the lenders of private money are not professional or business-oriented lenders unlike the moneylenders of hard money. Instead, they are individuals who are simply intending to achieve higher, yet, quicker returns on their cash.

Moreover, private money has usually lower loan points and fewer fees. The payment terms and duration can be both easily negotiable to serve the best interest of the parties. However, with private capital, expect that there are no fixed rules.

Investors typically use these loans when they believe they can easily raise the value of their property over a short period. In this way, they can handle the loan conveniently by refinancing their appreciated property and paying back the private lender in due time. Hence, similar with hard money, you should only use this loan when you have multiple and clearly defined exit strategies.

Home Equity Loan & Line of Credit | HELOC & HEIL

You can opt to access the equity in your primary residential property to help finance the acquisition of your other investment properties. Financial institutions and other established lenders can support you your intents of tapping into the equity you already have through financial products like the Home Equity Line of Credit (HELOC) or the Home Equity Installment Loan (HEIL).

To obtain your line of credit or home equity loan, you should first build equity in your home. Typically, banks will only lend you, in total, up to a specific percentage of the current value of your home. The percentage may differ between lenders, but you can find lending institutions can offer lending up to 90% of your home's value.

Actual Application Example: *Your current home is worth $200,000. You come to visit your local bank and found out that it can allow up to a maximum of 90% debt on your house. Hence, you can borrow a total loan of $180,000. If you already owe $80,000 on a first mortgage, the home equity line or loan caps it at $100,000, ensuring your total loans do not exceed 90%.*

Applying for either HELOC or HEIL has several more benefits compared to other conventional loans:

🏠 Lenders extend a loanable amount based on the prevailing value of your current primary residence, not on your newly purchased property. This implies that the lender would neither care about nor even get a peek on your new property, which can be in a terribly distressed condition. It has no concerns with whatever you might intend to spend with the loan, except your equity's capacity and your ability to repay it.

🏠 Since you can do whatever you wish with the money from a home equity line or loan, you can easily offer cash down payments when making offers on your new prospective properties. In this regard, you will have higher chances of acceptance for your offers.

🏠 Both HELOC and HEIL offer certain IRS-approved tax benefits like having the ability to deduct the interests paid on the loan. However, it would be better to confer with your CPA or attorney for further consultations on this matter.

🏠 Since the value of your primary residence actually secures the loan, the interest rates on either HELOC or HEIL are generally much lower than in hard or private money.

Another strategy often used by investors is to use a small bit of their home equity to fund the down payment on their investment property.

Real World Example: As an investor, you want to purchase an investment property for $200,000. However, you do not have the available cash down payment required for the acquisition but only the availability of a large equity in your own primary residence.

You already owe a total of $100,000 from existing mortgages of your other investment properties. Thus, for a 90% equity loan on your $300,000 residence, you can avail a maximum loan of $270,000 but with a cap of $170,000 after debts of your existing loans. You can then fund the usual 20%-down payment of $40,000 on your new investment property, and then, obtain from a bank a conventional mortgage for funding the remaining $160,000. You still have $130,000 left from the equity loan, which you can spare for acquiring more investment properties!

By the foregoing example, remember that your new investment properties are not entirely dependent on your equity loan. The technique is that you just have to be sure of continuously looking at your goals, schedules, and organizing your financial position before taking on a home equity product to further your real estate investing career.

Equity Partnership Agreement

Section 3 tapped briefly on the application of a business partnership, but it plainly discussed its aspect of structuring your real estate business entity. Another significant aspect of a business partnership in real estate investing is its financing ability.

For instance, if you desire to invest in a particular real estate, but its price range is just way outside your reach and guideline, an **equity partner** would simply be a great welcome addition to your property investing team. Equity partners can help you with great extents in financing your property deals.

You can structure a partnership in many ways—from using your partner to fund the down payment to using the resources of your partner to finance an entire investment property. With equity partnerships, there are no specific and set rules. You operate under previously agreed terms.

For each situation of invested deals, it requires its own proper evaluations. The evaluations include clear definitions on how to manage the specifics of the deal: administrative and financial operations, decision-making, active or passive role-playing, profit sharing scheme, and other pertinently significant details. Whatever final agreements reached on the operating procedures, both parties must sign the equity partnership agreement.

Typically, a partner receives a percentage of the ROI in accordance with the ownership/operating agreement. Depending on the agreement, the shared returns may include cash flow productions, appreciation, depreciation, and profits from exits.

Unlike private lending sources, equity partners do not receive any agreed upon interest rates on their financing funds. Instead, they receive a certain percentage of what the investment generates.

Obviously, shared returns will be higher whenever the investment produces more. Nevertheless, if it creates losses, equity partners may have to contribute further to keep the deal afloat.

Equity partners take higher risks than any private lending sources might; but, in return, they will have greater chances of earning significantly more whenever investment deals are successful. Additionally, unlike in a private lending scheme, a promissory or mortgage note does not secure the investment of equity partners, but by the operating agreement between the equity partners.

Commercial Lending

Although most of the aforementioned property-financing options primarily focus on the aspect of residential loans, commercial lending can also be a feasible option for your property investing activities. A commercial loan is what you will exactly need if you are simply planning to acquire real estate other than a single-unit or two- to four-unit residential properties.

Generally, commercial loans have slightly higher fees and interest rates. They also come mostly with shorter terms (usually, 90-day payment durations), require more loan points, and many different qualifying standards.

In commercial lending, it puts more emphasis on the assets of the borrower rather than the income, which residential lending focuses. The sustained logic in a commercial loan is that even if you own a $20-million apartment complex and things go haywire, you will never be able to meet the mortgage payment regardless of earning a high personal annual income.

While the commercial lender will still assess your income, credit rating, and other financial indicators, it just actually takes a picture of your financial skills. Yet, more importantly, in most cases, it focuses on the revenues that your properties generate.

In addition, commercial loans cover *'revolving lines of credit.'* A revolving loan may be either secured or unsecured by a mortgage or collateral. A borrower will draw down the line, even up to the maximum loan limit; and then, pays only a monthly interest.

After repaying the principal amount in full within the line's duration (usually, a year's period), the loan issuer can extend another line of credit to the borrower from year to year. If the borrower defaults, the loan issuer can no longer extend a line but rather convert it into a regular amortizing loan.

Revolving lines of credit are ideal to property investors, especially to flippers, who often have a reliable income that arrives at sporadic times; or, when they badly need funds in the meantime while awaiting the imminent sale of a property.

Apart from all these financing tools, you can also apply other forms of savings/investment products as financing instruments for your property investment requirements. These may include life insurance or equity indexed universal life (EIUL), Roth-individual retirement accounts (Roth-IRA), 401(k) plan, among others.

With so many of these financing vehicles to learn and keep in mind, you might still somehow take a ride towards the wrong financing route. Consider the following tips on the most common requirements you will fulfill in choosing your ride:

🏠 Depending on your paying capability, as well as your present and projected future earnings, decide on the specific type of mortgage loan to apply, which can best suit your situation and requirements. Take also into account its inclusive interest rates.

🏠 Review the loan agreement (preferably with your attorney), and always be aware of its terms and conditions, as well as other charges—fixed, floating, or hidden—levied by loan financiers.

🏠 When you hunt around for ideal deals, always exercise your bargaining powers while using a mortgage calculator for finding lower interest rates.

🏠 Lastly, is looking for the right mortgage insurance, which one of the most overlooked financing factor that caused many an investor to fumble. Search for insurers offering the lowest premiums!

"I had a couple come in with a negative amortization mortgage on a house that costs way too much relative to their income. They're consuming real estate, not investing in it."

—**Chris Cooper**, American Film Actor

8-Real Estate Marketing Tools & Strategies

"As soon as the land of any country has all become private property, the landlords, like all other men, love to reap where they never sowed, and demand a rent even for its natural produce."

—Excerpt from *'The Wealth of Nations'* by Scottish economist,
Adam Smith

Regardless of what choice of real estate investing niche, you decide to engage and be a master in, you would certainly need to apply marketing in any way, and to any extent. The concept of integrating a system of marketing in your business compels you to span outside of your regular spheres of influence and activities.

Growing your circles create much broader sets of dynamic and resource connections, which you should develop into a solid networking base. This base is the launching pad to catapult your business towards success.

Nevertheless, wherever you take your real estate investment business will be largely dependent on your system of marketing applications—ideas, skills, processes, tools, and strategies—and most especially, YOU!

Your Greatest Real Estate Marketing Tool: Yourself

Becoming the ultimate real estate investor, the primordial product you should be marketing is your personal brand—YOU! This does not cost you too much money; neither does it steal much of your time. Yet, if you ignore YOU, it costs you everything!

The moment you present yourself to the world and let people

know about yourself and what you do, you are actually starting to develop an impression, a reputation, a strong brand that you carry and build around you—your person!

Most of the time, you do not plan these self-presentations. They come spontaneously and you do not know when and where they happen that they catch you off guard. If you do, you will also never know where your conversations lead you.

Hence, you should always come prepared and guard your brand conscientiously. Learn how to market effectively your personal brand by inculcating the following virtues:

🏠 **Honesty:** if you are still starting and carving your niche in the real estate industry, you will not know about everything of its realm's breadths and depths; and that is just fine. For, after all, the fastest way to tarnish your reputation is right at the instance when you begin talking about things that you never actually know.

Never be what you are not. Do not ever misrepresent yourself. Never lie about your deals just to lure other investors. Dishonesty is a guarantee to never making any deals.

Most investors will immediately know any false pretenses you are putting up. Thus, they will quickly waste no time dealing with you any further. Worse, they will no longer do business with you. Worst, your dishonesty will spread like wildfire in the industry!

Admit and accept the things you do not know, and learn from them. Fact is that being inquisitive is a great way to grow as an investor/entrepreneur. Practice humility; listen intently to those who are more than willing to teach.

94

Integrity: Growing and nurturing your integrity is an unspoken invitation for all the people around you to keep them coming back to you, listening to you, patronizing you, and working with you, time after time. Keep sending this invitation; in turn, juicy deals will keep on inviting you!

The basic tenet for you to build and reach the highest levels of your integrity is to practice what you preach. Alternatively, practice the Golden Rule.

Learn that integrity is an essential element of your personal brand. Being an investor, the reputation you always carry precedes you wherever you may go.

Therefore, define and refine your mores. Adhere steadfastly to your ethical and moral codes of conduct, as well as the mores of your fellowmen and the rest of society.

You can never grow your business, much less, your personal brand if you do not keep your promises. You can never succeed if you keep pulling down others or putting one over them.

Even a solitary faux pas can tarnish easily your integrity. Hence, ensure showing continuously your integrity of the highest standards. Doing so will allow great businesses and opportunities finding you.

Professionalism: Act, think, and talk as a true professional for each relationship you build, each item you acquire, each appearance you bear, and each decision you make. In other words, look like a million dollars—just as your very promising property deal does—whenever, wherever, however, and whatever circumstances you get yourself along your way.

Your image is everything. It is a preview and a reflection of you and life's forthcoming attractions. Exhibit your personal brand with an exquisite professional image.

That also means spreading an exquisite professionalism even on the most mundane of things like the clothes you wear, the business cards you dispense, the look of your vehicle, the voicemail on all of your phones, and whatever. People always trust professionals; thus, always be one!

Marketing via Online & Offline Networking

No individual can ever succeed entirely without the help of others. People need people, and that is just how nature and the universe designed and willed it to be. Therefore, looking for the best people to collaborate with is much more important than looking for your deals.

"People facilitate properties to generate the moolah, never the other way around! Always remember, deals do not own people; people own deals! Properties are properties of people!"

To fulfill your urgent need for people, you simply ought to connect and interconnect, interact and establish these relationships with other people. In short, you need to network, meet, mingle, and know others for the simple purpose of creating mutual support or assistance towards moving one another forward.

Networking does not need to be a formal or methodical activity. Instead, your daily interactions with people should be integral to your networking strategy. Let networking be your lifestyle, your way of life!

The real estate industry, as always, has its own share of the good times and the bad times—the equally interesting rise and fall of fortunes. Back in 2006, just before the housing financial crisis, the membership of the National Association of Realtors (NAR) hit an all-time record high of a little below 1.5 million.

During and after the bursting of the housing bubble, however, it nosedived dramatically to its rock bottom of less than a million members in 2012. A rejuvenated membership had only picked up the slack a couple of years later; and since then, it has kept on increasing steadily, reaching 1.3 million members as of 2017.

Indeed, the current competition is becoming fiercer than ever. Nowadays, you ought to step up your efforts to survive and thrive, especially amidst the changing times and the fast-paced advancements in technological innovations.

Although real estate brokers/marketers remain the key players in the property buying process, property investors increasingly prefer performing more of the legwork on the Internet before associating with the gurus. According to a 2017 NAR study, more than 90% of investors use the Web to launch their property-hunting quest, creating the urgency for real estate brokers and marketers to engage in a more dynamic presence online.

If you are not engaging in an active networking online, then you are definitely missing out on half the life of the industry. To set yourself distinctively apart from the pack, you will just truly require both proficient online and offline real estate marketing skills and strategies. The following is a compilation of the most sensible real estate marketing ideas and strategies of the times to help you conquer the real estate marketing competition:

🏠 **Join a Real Estate Professional Investors' Community Club:** A property-investing club is an ideal venue to begin your offline networking and marketing activities. Investors congregate at these clubs regularly to discuss primarily the current investing strategies, market trends, the projected outlooks of the market, as well as looking out for the welfare of their fellows.

Other investors perhaps, only meet up at clubs for socials, trading horror stories of tenants, or simply, linking up with new colleagues or keeping in touch with old ones. Indeed, a club is not only a well of knowledge where you can learn quickly and continuously the ropes of the industry but also, a busy hive where you can build and grow your connections.

🏠 **Watch Closely the Entire Real Estate Marketing Competition:** Keep a watchful eye of what competitors do in the market (i.e., the ways of conducting their business dealings with buyers/ sellers, associates, or allied entities in the industry; the current appearances and activities on their websites; their movements and strategies in your area; their actions and exposures on social media, etc.). As much as possible, avoid committing their mistakes; rather, duplicate, if not, surpass their success!

🏠 **Be A Trailblazer and Carve Your Own Niche:** To follow or replicate others is good; to be different from the rest is better. If brewing marketing competition truly exists in your area, consider becoming a trailblazer and excelling at treading your path.

Make a name for yourself by establishing your expertise in a specific niche. Perhaps, you might want to stand out as the most trusted and reliable realtor for small families with toddlers, young urban professionals, divorcees, retirees, or whatever.

🏠 Design a Professionally Impressive Business Card: While most old-fashioned realty marketing aspects are fading away quickly, the business card remains an essential staple in the real estate industry. Create an awesome, professional-looking business card and dispense it around all your circles of influence.

🏠 Set Up and Establish Your Personal Brand Presence Online: Open the portal of the World Wide Web. Your entry leads you to vast fields of networking and marketing opportunities—social media, online community forums, communication apps, the blogosphere, and what have you.

Explore and exploit these free networking and marketing services to the greatest possible advantage with respect to your property-investing career. Foremost, ensure creating your social media accounts on all the giant networking sites (i.e., Facebook, Google+, Pinterest, Twitter, Tumbler, and even Instagram or Vero if you take countless snapshots of houses/properties).

You need not be present at most times on every network; focusing on a single or a couple is much better than becoming non-existent on all sites. Be constantly active in your sites by interacting regularly with users, posting your activities, promoting your properties, and sharing good press, contents, or emotional stories with compelling copies and powerful audio/visual elements.

Remember, social media is all about creating and building relationships. Therefore, beware of using it as your advertising platform. Your networking trick should rather be spending a portion of your time growing solid relationships while making an impression of yourself as someone with knowledge in your craft.

If you want to advertise, include social media paid ads in the saddle. Dish out a budget for social media paid ads like Facebook ads, which are generally the most effective channel to get in front of your target audience.

🏠 **Participate In Real Estate Investing Community Forums:** Similar to community clubs, these forums are online communities participated by professional realtors and realty investors. They network with one another at all times of the day. Usually, their networking activities are about sharing relevant and significant information about the market/industry, as well as helping one another to learn, grow, and prosper.

It is noteworthy that networking in these forums must never be about what you can get something out of them, but rather, how you can contribute to the conversations. Thus, you can help yourself learn by just reading between the lines of the dialogues.

🏠 **Create and Develop an Outstanding Website:** Most consumers nowadays prefer doing the bulk of the legwork themselves online whenever they make major decisions on purchasing various products or availing specific services (which both include buying real estate and using realty services). Take their cue; build one!

Owning a website reflects professionalism and seriousness of doing business in the industry. Not only will your business website address the needs of people but also, it serves your interests in networking and marketing your business.

Building a great website is neither difficult nor expensive. Being terrible at technology is not a valid excuse in today's technology-friendly world. You should only brush up more on user experience (UX) design skills rather than site architecture technology.

Essentially, your site is your storefront to your business. Thus, it must require looking spic and span, professional, organized, easy to navigate, mobile-friendly, and alluring to attract more people flocking to your site. Make everything simple but sleek.

In your site, you should create irresistible contents that offer to capture your prospects or leads. Ensure your copy to include locally oriented keywords so that homebuyers searching online in your area can run across your content.

You should also add the pertinent social sharing buttons on your site. Home shoppers are always more than eager to share top picks of housing pics with their family and friends.

Lastly, you should make yourself easily available and contacted. Ideally, create an attention-grabbing 'contact us' page on your site; also, place your contact details on every page in your site.

🏠 **Build Your *'Google My Business'* Website:** Attract new sets of clientele and opportunities with a free business listing by setting up your Google My Business website. Your listing is a location-based page that appears right down people's alley when they search for businesses or services like yours on both Google Search and Google Maps.

Usually, homebuyers will use Google Map to search the address of a property and view the property's photos. They will also use the map's Street View feature to get a feel of the locality, see the proximities of landmarks, businesses, or places of interests, and more ideally, take on a virtual tour of the entire property. Hence, always have the user experience in mind by ensuring their easy access to all the aforementioned information to your page. Ensure also to have great eye-catching photos and smooth virtual tours.

🏠 Get Aboard on Pinterest Boards: Optimize your activity at Pinterest by creating Pinterest boards. They are most useful for providing high-resolution images and comprehensive visual information about your specific property listings.

🏠 Immerse in Commerce with Zillow: Zillow is the leading online real estate marketplace, where you can connect with other local investors and realty professionals. Actually, it is the Yelp (a hosting site that publishes crowd-sourced reviews on various local businesses, as well as offering advertising and online reservation services) of real estate marketing.

At Zillow, you can search for your most desired deals from its humongous database, which contains infinite numbers of rental and for-sale listings. You can also compare property values by using the site's property valuation tool, Zestimate.

Zillow also offers abilities to advertise your properties and being an agent on their site. This could somehow be a bit pricey, but taking into account the enormous role Zillow plays in the industry, it is certainly your best bet. For, after all, the site accounts for more than 50% online traffic for all searches about real estate.

Like Yelp, Zillow allows its users to review and rate real estate agents. Hence, wear your best smile and keep on racking up your rating. Solid star-ratings will greatly help to increase your leads, as well as capturing them to close a deal.

🏠 Apply A Leveraged Call-Tracking System: Most property buyers reach over the telephone when availing the services of a realtor or placing an appointment to inspect a property. Usually, these calls arise from your paid search campaigns (i.e., social media paid ads or pay-per-click ads).

From these calls and their transpired conversations, you will be able to track or know which of your ads or the keywords you use are driving all these calls. Apply this call-tracking system to devise and develop your real estate marketing funnel.

🏠 **Execute Marketing via Direct Mail/Email:** Regardless if you are buy-and-hold, flipper, or wholesaler, your investing business relies not only on looking for great deals but also on having a steady supply of prospects for those deals. For a huge number of investors, direct mailing is their primary source of leads.

Mailing, either direct or electronic, is simply sending letters, newsletters, postcards, etc. to these targeted prospects, with the hope that a certain percentage of the recipients respond. The concept of mail campaigns is to let your audience build an awareness of your brand, business, product, or service over the course of time. A response could lead you to be the ultimate solution to their pressing needs.

Build your mailing list either by procuring public records from your local assessor or hiring an online outfit (i.e., ListSource). Obtaining public records is free while using an online service can save you time; hence, keep your objectives in mind when creating your mailing list.

In addition, never fail to include in your list those absentee property owners, as well as owners of abandoned properties, apartment buildings, pre-foreclosed or foreclosed properties, expired listings, and *'probates'* (properties undergoing distribution or transfer to heirs of the deceased owner). More often than not, these types of property owners will be leading you to fantastic opportunities and land great deals.

They neither want to hold on any longer with their assets or care about spending and maintaining their properties. As a result, they just wish to sell their properties at a discount.

With a changing market, update your list every six months to rid out those unresponsive ones while giving room for new leads. The frequency by which you send your mail and the duration of your campaign varies depending on the marketing funnel you set up and the investing method you are engaging.

🏠 **Exercise Post-Closing Marketing Techniques:** Your relationships with your clients must be never-ending, even after a close. Let them remember you, your service, and the entire fruitful experience shared.

You may send them a local care package or restaurant gift cards or theater or movie tickets, etc. Always stay in touch with your past buyers to maintain goodwill. You may send greeting cards, holiday or anniversary cards, etc. to help them recall you.

Never mind the cost; do not even perceive it as public relations tactics. Instead, mind to share your blessings. Besides, your main intent is making them remember your person and personal brand. These items are just a minuscule of the overflowing returns ahead like continuing business deals or precious referrals.

Testimonials from previous clients are tremendous trust signals. Find ways to let them endorse you without soliciting directly. Real people supporting and showing your services to the world is an indirect marketing to gain more potential clients. Make the most out of these testimonials and endorsements by posting them strategically on your site while sharing them every now and then on social media networks.

As you may see, the ideas aforementioned are not expansive and do not even include other options possible. Fact is that an entire book can cover each marketing concept and technique. Nonetheless, the book presents you with the most commonly used real estate marketing strategies today.

The real estate marketing process is not really a simple and smooth-sailing activity. One important aspect to keep in mind, especially when you are still getting started, is to put your focus on just a single or a couple of marketing strategies. Work hard to implement them carefully. At the same time, monitor the results.

As soon as you found what worked out, stick with it. If you plan to generate more leads, try to expand your newfound successful strategy. Alternatively, move on to practice another marketing technique.

Just the same, not all real estate marketing strategies produce effective results. For this reason, your vital key is to maintain accurate records and test continuously your marketing campaigns.

"Every day, you will have opportunities to take chances and to work outside your safety net. Sure, it is a lot easier to stay in your comfort zone... In my case, business suits and real estate... but sometimes, you have to take risks. When the risks pay off, that is when you reap the biggest rewards."

—Donald Trump

9-The Art of Unloading Your Real Estate Investment: Moving Ahead

"Everyone wants a piece of land. It is the only sure investment. It can never depreciate like a car or a washing machine. Land doubles its value in ten years...or in less than that...land is appreciating every day."

—**Sam Shepard**, American Playwright & Actor

Real estate investing is a great means to a great end—passive wealth building! In the fullness of time, your invested property produces a cash flow that would earn you a substantial income while steadily gaining an intense equity, and hopefully, appreciation.

Some property investors decide to choose to hold on to their investments within an indefinite duration before finally unloading them for a profit. Others will simply find no intentions of unloading their properties, but rather, find contentment by holding on to these steadily cash-flowing properties until fate unloads their lives from this world.

Nevertheless, at one point in your investing journey, you will most likely decide to choose unloading one or a couple or more of your properties due to various reasons. The ensuing issue thereon is to choose the best strategy for unloading or exiting your real estate investment. Your exit strategy choice is as important as your previous decision of purchasing the involved investment. Learn the following exit strategies you may use today or in the future:

Exiting Thru Real Estate Agents

Oftentimes, a real estate agent will cost you an additional 6% to sell the property for you. For an overview of liquidating the extra fee, a responsible real estate agent will typically perform the following tasks for you (refer to Image-6):

Advertise the sale of your property (the least is by word-of-mouth and placing a sign in strategic premises of your property).

List your property on the MLS, usually accessed by all real estate agents across the country.

Show your property to prospective buyers.

Market your property to the best of his/her abilities through networking, Craigslist, LoopNet, and other online or offline marketing strategies.

Lead and manage the negotiations with potential purchasers.

Handle all the legwork and paperwork of the purchase process.

Image-6: Basic Duties of a Hired Real Estate Agent for Property Exiting Services

Within the spheres of real estate agents, the **'80/20 rule'** or the **'Pareto principle'**—the natural law of the vital few stating that about 80% of the effects arise from 20% of the causes—would oftentimes hold true. That is, only 20% of real estate agents can sell successfully 80% of the listings!

Therefore, if you intend to list your property with an agent, it is very important to find one from that 20% vital few and let him/her pursue working his/her magic. Searching from this elite bunch requires you to interview several agents so you can pick whom you might feel most comfortable to collaborate with to get your property sold in less than no time.

After you have chosen your agent, you will thereafter enter and agree to a contract, giving your agent the authority to represent you and earn the 6%-commission after selling the property. Usually, you and your buyer split the fee to pay the agent who brought in the buyer. In cases where your selling agent represents both you and your buyer, you will pay the entire commission fee to the agent.

However, this commission rate may slightly change, depending on the type of your property, its location, and price. You will be deciding the price of your property before your agent lists it on the MLS.

Pricing is crucial since you do not want to be listing your property too high (which may lead to extending your holding time) or too low (which may be leaving money on the table). A reliable agent must be able to look at pricing comparisons of other similar properties or perform broker comps to determine the best selling price to list it.

Many investors feel that this preliminary transaction with an agent completes their role in selling the property, and then, let their agent handle everything from thereon. This should never be the case.

As the seller, you will have many more techniques and tricks you can do to ensure your property will sell for the highest amount and at the soonest possible time. Begin tweaking the interior and exterior appearances of your property to be more desirable.

Compare your property against similarly comparable properties, and target yours to make it look better than the competition. Once you receive an offer, the exciting negotiations begin (refer to stages 8 to 10 of the property purchasing process)

Exiting Thru 'For-Sale-By-Owner (FSBO)' Process

For some investors, the costs of hiring a real estate agent are simply too high for them. Hence, they rather choose to sell their property via the for-sale-by-owner (FSBO) selling option.

In this case, and without the services of an agent, you cannot list your property on the MLS. This will somehow be a major limiting factor to exit your property. You will lose the ability to span across the vast majority of property buyers.

Nonetheless, you can use the latest tool—'Flat Fee MLS Listing Service,'—applied by some FSBO sellers. The servicing tool requires you (the seller) to pay a flat fee to a real estate agent to list your property in the MLS.

Typically, the flat fee ranges from $150 to $400. Yet, this fee only involves a very limited assistance from your agent.

Your agent's responsibility is to simply execute the first two duties (refer to Image-6) for servicing the exit. This leaves you to perform all the rest of the supposed duties of your agent.

In addition, since a sale of property transaction includes both the seller's agent and the buyer's agent, you will still be paying a commission to whose agent brings in the buyer to the deal. Hence, you end up paying 3% out of pocket.

Exiting Thru 'Carrying-the-Contract' Method

Real estate investors interchange the property exit term, carrying-the-contract, with *'seller financing.'* Seller financing is the practice of a property seller to carry some, or all of the debts, necessary to buy the property. Meaning, instead of going through financial intermediaries like banks, both the buyer and the seller conclude the transaction in a manner where the buyer makes payments on the property directly to the seller at an agreed upon interest rate.

On one hand, seller financing is commonly the last resort of other investors-buyer-borrowers who cannot obtain financing elsewhere or qualify for a regular mortgage loan. This property selling method is advantageous for the investors-buyer-borrowers since the agreed-upon interest rate is typically much lower than a bank imposes.

On the other hand, seller financing is also commonly the last resort of other investors-sellers who are unable to sell their properties without offering it to buyers who are unable to obtain financing. This property selling method is, likewise, advantageous for the investors-sellers since they can receive higher returns on the sale since they no longer have to pay any incurred selling costs to the financial intermediary.

Additionally, investors-sellers in seller financing can receive monthly income that no longer involves issues of the concerned property such as maintenance works, rentals, or tenants. Upon the consummation of the sale, the new buyer will ultimately own full responsibility to the property, including ownership rights and

111

its ensuing issues and expenses (maintenance, insurance, taxes, etc.).

Essentially, therefore, seller financing can be a win-win solution for both the seller and the buyer; or, property investors.

Nevertheless, there are foreseen risks in seller financing. The largest of which is when your buyer defaults payments at some point. As that event arises, you will have no other choice but to foreclose the property and void the buyer's rights.

Consequently, you are subject to undergo the foreclosure process and institute the laws similarly imposed by a lending institution. Obviously, this will take much of your time and money. Foreclosure rules for each locality can vary to certain extents; so, you will most likely need your attorney to handle and get through the entire foreclosure process.

After completing the foreclosure, you will be getting back your property and the chance of selling it all over again. Apparently, you have to be dealing deal with some issues or repairs before your property is ready for selling again.

Although the risks of foreclosing your property can be inevitable, you can lessen the risks if you can manage the financing note properly. Hence, you should have to screen your prospective buyer carefully so you will be fully aware of the issues that might arise.

Moreover, another ideal way to reduce the risks is to require a hefty and non-refundable cash down payment so you can protect your interest. A large up-front payment can prevent the possibility of your buyer to default on the monthly payments.

In addition, it is noteworthy that you must go through the normal procedures of the purchasing process, using an attorney or a title/escrow company, and all the pertinent legal paperwork, in order to assure the proper performance of the sale.

Exiting Thru the Lease-Option Agreement

When applying the lease-option exit strategy, you should know the separate twin components of its arrangement:

🏠 *'The Lease:'* Executing the lease-option component is similar to any other property leased out, wherein your tenant will move into your property and make the required rental payments.

🏠 *'The Option:'* This option, which is in the form of a legal agreement, gives the legal right to your tenant for purchasing your property within a pre-determined tenancy period at a pre-determined price. Hence, such option will make it illegal for you (property owner) to sell your property during the pre-determined tenancy period. In return for your tenant's option to be the sole buyer of your property, your tenant must pay a non-refundable *'option fee'* up front. You will apply this upfront fee later towards the purchase.

Therefore, in the very simplest of terms, a lease-option is a regular lease with the option to purchase. Both investors negotiating the terms of a lease-option agreement should consider the following (refer to Image-7):

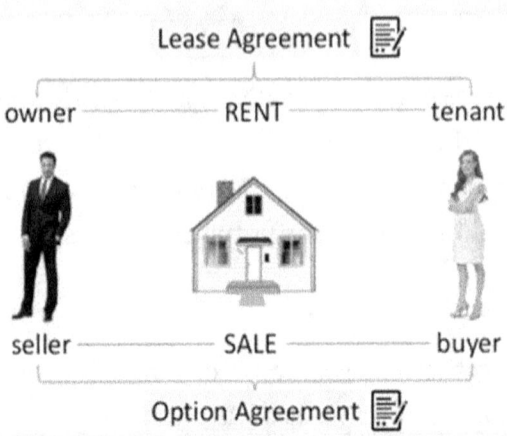

Laying Down the Specifics: *Will it be granting an OPTION (the right to buy, even if the seller later changes his/her mind and does not wish to sell to anyone at all), or a RIGHT-OF-FIRST-REFUSAL (the right to buy if or when the owner ever decides to sell)?*

Pre-Determined Tenancy Duration: *What are the earliest and the latest due dates for exercising the option?*

Lease Renewal/Extension: *Renewals are new leases. Extensions are continuations of old leases. If the option is applicable at any time during the lease term, does it continue if there is a renewal or an extension of the lease?*

Reassignment of the Option: *Can the tenant sell the option to another entity without assigning a lease (Sell Wholly)? If not, may the tenant, at least, sell the option to another entity in which the tenant is still a controlling or 100% shareholder (Reassign the Lease)?*

Pricing Agreement: *Will the parties agree to a fair market value or agree to a formula that employs some index that is independent and easily verifiable?*

Pricing Agreement: *Will the parties agree to a fair market value or agree to a formula that employs some index that is independent and easily verifiable?*

Termination of the Option: *What events will allow the property owner to terminate the option, even if the lease continues?*

Image-7: Investor's Guidelines for Specific Terms & Conditions of a Lease-Option Agreement

Exiting Thru Tax Deferment & Reinvestment: 1031-Exchange

With your real estate investing business venture, the government always exercises its duty to collect its share from your gains. If you sell your property, you will certainly incur significant due payment of taxes (i.e., capital gains tax).

Fortunately, if you are a taxpayer, the government provides a legal way, or a breather, for you to defer those due taxes to a later time. Essentially, this is the desirable effort or supportive way of the government to collaborate with you on your property investment deals.

However, you need to follow a number of set rules to avail this tax deferment or temporary exemption of paying your taxes. When done properly, you can possibly reuse the intended tax payments as available funds for your next deal.

Under Section 1031 of the U.S. Internal Revenue Code, the '*1031 Exchange*' gives you (seller) the ability to exchange like-kind property while deferring to pay the taxes on the realized gains. Under normal circumstances, if a buyer purchases your property for $10,000 but exchanges it for $100,000 in cash, you gain $90,000, upon which you must pay the gains tax.

Yet, due to §1031, if you exchange your property for a like-kind property, then there will be a realized gain (meaning, it occurs) but not recognized (meaning, no taxes will be due at that time). The property you gave up is the relinquished property; while the property you received is the replacement property. After the consummation of the exchange, the basis in the relinquished asset will also become the basis of the replacement asset.

Therefore, the purchase price of your relinquished property for $10,000, called the *'basis,'* becomes the basis of the replacement property. When you sell the replacement property later for $150,000, then your gain would be $140,000 (that is, $150,000 less $10,000, and not $150,000 less $100,000).

That is absolute unless you perform another 1031 exchange at that time. You will currently have no limit on how many exchanges you can perform in a lifetime.

The property or properties exchanged must be categorically qualifying properties of usage, or used for income producing purposes such as rental or for investment, or used in a business or trade. Hence, vacation homes and personal residences are not qualifying properties.

Swapping of properties, on the other hand, is a very useful tax instrument. However, it could relatively be rare finding property owners wanting to exchange properties amidst a simultaneous closing. In effect, the IRS allows the usage of a *'fiction,'* a sort of like-kind property proxy.

In the fiction, you may sell your property for cash, but you must place the money in escrow to hold. This indicates that you will have no fingerprints on the money; neither you can spend it nor borrow against it.

You shall then have only 45 days to identify a certain replacement property and complete filling out the identification information form. Subsequently, you will just have a short time closing on the identified replacement property, using the funds held in escrow. If done exactly right, you can then defer the tax payment.

More precisely, you defer paying the capital gains taxes until reselling the property with no intentions of reinvestment. Investors commonly use the tax-free 1031 exchanges whenever they sell their property with the intention of using the proceeds to purchase a similar asset.

Nevertheless, there are actually more complications going into a 1031-exchange. Thus, ensure to consult with your CPA or a qualified tax specialist prior to making your final decision.

You should now have a better understanding of how to get out eventually of your real estate investments. Remember: every step of your way must begin with your end in mind. This way, you will always make it much easier for you to unload your investment and clear a much more fulfilling profit!

"The right to private property meant at the same time the right and duty to be personally concerned about your own well-being, to be personally concerned about your family's income, to be personally concerned about your future. This is hard work."

—**Mikhail Khodorkovsky**, Russian Oligarch & Philanthropist

Realities of Realties Investing: A Conclusion

"He is not a full man who does not own a piece of land."

—Hebrew Proverb

The objective of any investing venture—and that includes real estate investing—is to buy low and sell high. This is a simple practice and mantra that makes real estate investing even more alluring and worth trying.

The beauty of it all, there is always a clear chance that a property could raise its value just as there are probabilities that values might decline. Investing in real estate is indeed a thrilling activity that provides you with vast opportunities to create an enormous passive wealth, and perhaps, build your investment empire.

By their fluctuating values, together with its rise and fall of huge fortunes, the real estate market has become an approximate barometer for a nation's entire economy. That means to say that the economy might be in a pleasant and stable standing when the value of real estate appreciates; conversely, it could be teetering when property values depreciate.

Regardless of the intrinsic variability of a property's value—and perhaps, those frightening experiences from past property meltdowns—the real estate industry has always been growing steadily through the years. People, as well as realty investors, are learning more each day about how to search for their ideal real estate; finance to acquire it; manage and care for it; and ultimately, marketing to sell it at planned and windfall profits!

More than ever, property investors are beginning to discover and recognize how the market functions vis-à-vis the current laws that bound it and the rapidly changing times that it has to adapt. They even explore more just to scour or create leveraged systems out of the limiting factors that restrict the movements of the market.

The government is aware of these enterprising activities. Thus, while it realizes the significant link between real estate and the economy, government continuously finds ways to create slacks on taxation to support the industry. In effect, investors are now able to identify and enjoy various tax benefits of property investing.

The World Wide Web also contributes its own share for the thriving realty industry. The Internet keeps on facilitating a huge part of the population in joining the bandwagon of investing in real estate. Investors are now able to search for desired properties through a host of various websites. Even those reality-TV shows promoting property investing are chipping in to propel the industry towards reaching newer heights and glories.

With all these assistance, a stable state of the economy, and the influx of would-be investors, the real estate market today has only become tougher than ever, nonetheless. The competition among both realtors and investors is fiercer than it ever was.

Homeowners are scooping up single-family housing units, attempting to acquire their next house before mortgage interest rates rise. Novice investors are feeling perpetually thrilled and excited about the perceived and actual powers of real estate investing that they are racking up continuously to purchase most 'nasty, decrepit, and hopeless' properties, including those small multi-family deals.

Giant institutional investors and hedge funds are both racing up against each other to grab all the larger and sweeter apartment deals at prices that simply do not make any sense to realty gurus and industry-savvy investors.

In the end, real estate investors all find themselves having a choice: either they sit it out and keep waiting for the next big real estate bubble to burst or they activate their creativities to look for excellent opportunities in today's market. Of course, nothing is ever wrong with sitting it out for the next few years, but apparently, you must love the action too much to stop!

Investing in properties can always be worthwhile, only if you manage it correctly and you have a good grasp of the imminent signs in the market. Your potentials to create and grow sizeable profits could be unlimited, for as long as you keep taking into account each of the market factors.

In summary, real estate investments present an enticing profile of a high-value risk-return nature. Hence, thoughtful considerations of the all the sections discussed in this manual will enable you to reap the great benefits while mitigating the lurking risks.

You just ought to have a clear vision why real estate investing can and shall be your most significant step towards growing wealth for you and your family's future.

THE CRUX OF THE MATTER IS SIMPLY HAVING A SOLID FOUNDATIONAL REAL ESTATE INVESTMENT PLAN!

This is what the entire guideline is all about, and outlined for you! Others failed primarily due to deficient planning and preparations. Fall not into this trap! Land on land!

"Real estate is an imperishable asset, ever increasing in value. It is the most solid security that human ingenuity has devised. It is the basis of all security and about the only indestructible security."

—**Russell Sage**, American Politician & Financier

www.ingramcontent.com/pod-product-compliance
Lightning Source LLC
Chambersburg PA
CBHW071324220526
45468CB00001B/490